101 THINGS

EVERY MAN SHOULD KNOW HOW TO DO

101
THINGS

EVERY MAN SHOULD KNOW HOW TO DO

Design: Paul Peddrick (cover), John Mitrione (interior)

WEbook, Inc.
307 Fifth Avenue, 7th Floor
New York, NY 10016
646.453.8575
www.WEbook.com

ISBN: 978-1-935003-04-5

Library of Congress Cataloging-in-Publication Data has been applied for.

Printed in the United States.

Cover images: Wood background © Siede Preis/Photodisc/Getty Images; whiskey on the rocks © iStockphoto.com/ Sergei Didyk; playing cards © David Toase/Photodisc/Getty Images; diamond ring © Thomas Northcut/Photodisc/ Getty Images; napkin (front and back) © Siri Stafford/Digital Vision/Getty Images; matchbook (front and back) © David Toase/Photodisc/Getty Images; bear © Stockbyte/Getty Images; passport © ballyscanlon/Digital Vision/Getty Images; cigar © C Squared Studios/Photodisc/Getty Images; fork © iStockphoto.com/Ryan Balderas; dollar bill © iStockphoto.com/Paul Paladin.

101 THINGS
EVERY MAN SHOULD KNOW HOW TO DO

SECTION II: THE IMPRESSIVE MAN

SECTION III: THE TRICKY MAN

SECTION IV: THE RESOURCEFUL MAN

ABOUT THE AUTHORS

For Charles Bronson, Cosmo
Kramer, Inspector Gadget, Hector
"Macho" Comacho, MacGyver, and
all the other men who have shown
us the way...

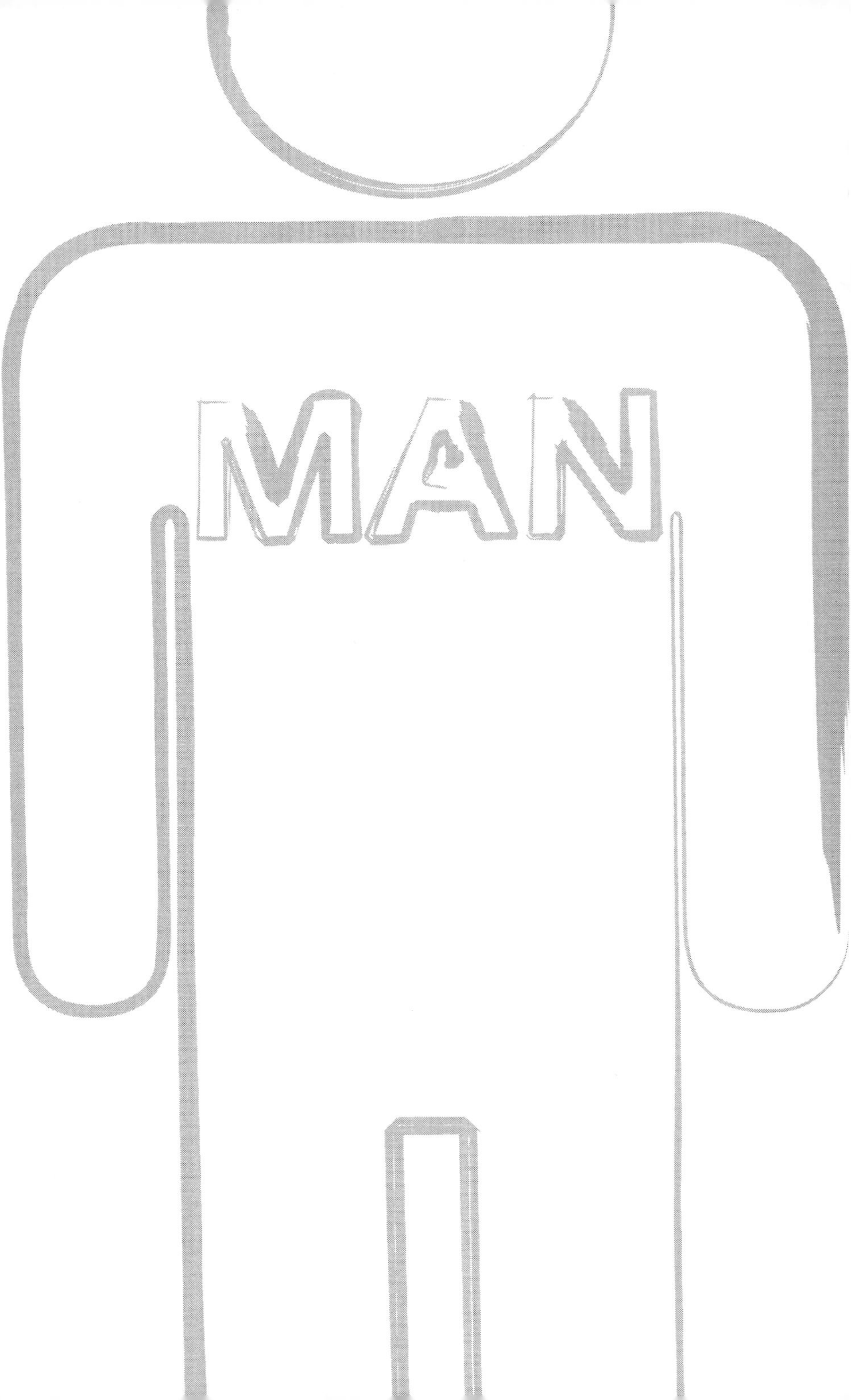
MAN

INTRODUCTION

By William Tiernan

Two or three times a year, I get together with a few college buddies to play golf, drink a few beers, and smoke cigars. Inevitably, we end up making lists: top 10 albums of all time; best Major League ballparks; favorite Al Pacino movies; beautiful women with whom we've struck out. (The latter list fills up quickly.)

On a recent trip, standing on the fourth tee of some obscure golf course in Virginia, I posed the question that is the fountainhead of this book: "What are the definitive things all guys should be able to do?"

Chuck took a swig of his Miller Light tall boy. "Burp the alphabet."

Tim puffed on the $2.99 cigar he got at 7-11. "Be good at least one sport."

Matt teed up his ball and smacked it with his Taylor Made R7 SuperQuad. "Hit a golf ball 300 yards," he grunted.

I watched his ball fly deep into the woods. "Shouldn't it have to go straight?" I asked.

"Nope," he said. "Three hundred yards in *any* direction is manly enough." He bent to pick up his tee, and added, "And fix stuff. Guys have to be able to fix stuff."

Guys love lists. We love them because we are competitive and enjoy ranking things. But what about a list dedicated to ourselves? What about a list that highlights all the things we should be able to do— things that define who we are, and separate us from those who like to garden. Through the years, my dad has taught me a few of these things, like how to bait a fishing hook with a blood worm and drive a stick shift. But being a man in today's society requires more than basic skill. How should we, for example, plan a romantic vacation? Or perfect the art of foreplay? Or look good in a Speedo? Or win a fight quickly and easily? The challenge here is not simply to list things guys should be able to do; we know we *should* able to make a decent bowl of chili, avoid doing chores, and pull off the perfect marriage proposal. But we don't always know *how*.

We need a guide, similar to the hulking "Life Science" textbook we got in seventh grade…only 300 pages shorter, with essays, explanations, charts, and diagrams we can reference when we need to plan a romantic vacation for our leading lady. Maybe something called *101 Things Every Man Should Know How to Do*?

Exactly.

This book is *the* essential guide to being a man in the twenty-first century. It's diverse enough to teach us how to play beer pong like a pro, how to listen without listening, and how to escape an alien abduction. Now, if you're looking for a guide that will help you plant seasonal shrubs, *101 Things* is not for you. But if you want to save your neon-green Budweiser bar sign from a trip to the garbage, or give a killer best-man speech, or perfect the art of apologizing for being unapologetic, this guide will show you how. Simply put, *101 Things* is for men who want to indulge, fight, impress women, get away with anything, and be all-around resourceful, capable studs.

Want to cook the perfect steak? Andrew Gori lays it out for you. Need to ass-whoop a bear? Ryan Placchetti offers a step-by-step analysis. Want to get ripped and be sexy? Steve Chang chisels out a solution in just a few easy steps! Itching to sneak into Cuba? John Meils tells you how. From the practical to the absurd, from the sensitive to the sublime, the golden nuggets of *101 Things* are designed to help all guys not only get through their days, but excel in the race up the ladder of manliness.

My dad also taught me to stand up when a lady approaches your dinner table and never wear jean shorts. While these pearls of wisdom have helped me impress my grandmother and stave off a life dedicated to NASCAR, dad didn't teach me how to get out of a speeding ticket, execute the perfect bribe, date two girls at the same time, fix anything, avoid going to the Laundromat, or buy a used car. Reading *101 Things Every Man Should Know How to Do* teaches you all of these critical skills—and more.

As an added bonus scattered throughout this book, you'll find the sage advice of Mr. Man, our resident Ph.D. in all things manly. Mr. Man receives hundreds of letters a day from disgruntled and frustrated men: Men whose wives ask them repeatedly if they are fat; men who can't fix toilets and broken door handles; and men who drink too much milk in public. If you're a man with a problem, Mr. Man has the answer. He's tough, funny, and a trusted friend in difficult situations.

So plop yourself in your beer-stained La-Z-Boy, tell your buddy to fetch you a cold one, flip on your flat-screen for reruns of *The Man Show*, and grab your copy of *101 Things Every Man Should Know How to Do*. We've broken it down into four easy-to-digest sections: Manly Man, Impressive Man, Tricky Man, and Resourceful Man. With submissions ranging from light and breezy to downright outrageous, from in-depth essays to inspirational one-shots, *101 Things* has something for everyone. And who knows? If you've got a bad case of diarrhea from a Friday-night bender, you could learn everything there is to know about being a man, all in one sitting.

SECTION I:

THE MANLY MAN

Essential Knowledge for the Bold and Brawny

#1: FIGHT A BEAR

By Ryan Placchetti

Before I begin, my lawyer informs me that I should mention that I have never actually fought a bear. However, I feel I have license to speak on the matter for the same reason that scientists are permitted to postulate on the far reaches of space without going there. If you can accept that stars are burning balls of gas trillions of miles away, there's no reason to doubt my advice when squaring off against a fearsome predator. After all, bears are much closer to us than stars—Ursas Major and Minor notwithstanding.

Note that this is not a survival guide. In fact, it's likely the opposite. Supposedly, the best way to "survive" a bear attack is to lie down and play dead. It's also the best way to look like a wimp during what could be the defining moment of your life as a man. Feel free to give up, but don't come crying to me when your friends heckle you for the rest of your life. It's your own fault for being a wuss. But if you fight and die, you could be the dude who bit it after cold-cocking a bear. This would ensure immortality at your local watering hole. ("Watering hole" is, of course, man-slang for a place that doesn't serve water.)

Know Your Enemy

If you're going to fight a bear, there are a few things you ought to know first—not that any of this should make a lick of difference, if you're a real man.

Gentrification

Don't be fooled by pop culture's softening of the bear persona. They are not cute and fluffy stuffed animals; they are natural-born killing machines. No matter how you dress them—even though a female bear might start to look good in a tutu or a tube top after you've had a few beers, grinding on a tree like a stripper pole—you're not going to want to take one home at the end of the night. Case closed.

SPECIES

Not all bears are created equal. You don't have to be a certified mechanic to know the difference between a Ford F150 and a Mazda B-Series. One is going to haul the load, and the other is going to get you beat up at a truck rally. They're both pickups, but they're not playing in the same arena. With that in mind, I'd like to introduce you to some of the bears you might encounter in combat. They've been ordered from greatest to least, in terms of how much man-cred you can expect to receive for taking one down:

The Polar Bear. These giants can weigh over 1,500 pounds, and you'll probably have to travel to the inhospitable ice floes north of the eighty-eighth parallel to find one—unless you just go to your local zoo. The polar bear is the only bear that is completely carnivorous. That makes it the biggest, meat-eating land mammal on Earth. Did I mention that male polar bears don't hibernate? In other words, these killers never sleep, which means sneaking up on one during a long winter nap is out of the question. Also, you wouldn't be able to because these behemoths are like the special forces of the bear nation, sweet tatts and all. To clarify, they don't really have tattoos. There's nothing you can draw on a polar bear to make it scarier.

The Brown Bear. This group's best-known contender is the grizzly. A male brown bear can weigh up to 1,500 pounds, so you're really going to want to bring your kung-fu, grasshopper. They're plentiful in North America, but your best chance of catching one with his pants down is in Russia, where more than half of them make their homes amid the plentiful gulags and vodka distilleries. They don't hibernate either—because they're wasted all the time.

The Black Bear. This is your run-of-the-mill, trash-eating bear. With sub-species in Asia and North America, the odds are that if you're fighting a bear, it's going to be one of these suckers. There are estimated to be more than 800,000 black bears in North America alone. However, because they only weigh in between a paltry 250 pounds to a mediocre 600 pounds, fighting a black bear isn't going to mean squat if someone else you know has fought a grizzly. If you really want to know what you're made of, upgrade to a bigger bear, or fight two at the same time.

The Sloth Bear. These natives of the Indian sub-continent barely count as bears at all. Weighing up to 310 pounds is no great feat in the bear community, relatively speaking (polar bears take dumps bigger than that). Don't underestimate the sloth bear though, as they are characterized by their long claws and aggressive temperament. In fact, they are more feared than the tiger in their homelands. (Keep in mind also that the most famous tigers in the world have been tamed by men wearing spandex and sequins.)

The Giant Panda. The name of this group is incredibly misleading. So-called "giant" pandas can weigh up to 250 pounds, which might be intimidating if you're a starving Chinese peasant. However, at that measly size, a giant panda wouldn't last five minutes on the defensive line of the Chicago Bears. They do have thumbs though, so guard against grabs, joint locks, and fishhook techniques in a rumble.

The Sun Bear. The sun bear is the Mazda pickup of the bear family. They typically weigh no more than 145 pounds and are frequently kept as pets, due to their amiable personalities and exceptionally long tongues. In short, this bear is a waste of any real man's time. However, if you put a sun bear in a wading pool filled with banana pudding, you'll probably attract strippers. Something about large quantities of pudding makes them scrappy. Now that's a fight worth seeing.

Before Doing Battle

Like any great warrior going into battle, you need to steel yourself. You need to collect all of your guts, get drunk, and write out your last will and testament...not necessarily in that order.

Scenarios

There are a few ways you might find yourself locked in battle with a bear:

1. You're in the woods minding your own business. Maybe you're camping, hiking, or just-plain lost because you were too cocky to ask for directions—all of which, in my humble opinion, are perfectly legitimate reasons to find yourself in the wild. You're doing your thing, and a bear shows up trying to start a ruckus. You reach down, find your cojones, and resolve to guard the honor of your species.

2. You decide to a do a little breaking and entering, eat some porridge, bust up some furniture, and take a nap. Then, the owner comes home. Surprise! It's a freakin' bear! He's not going to let you get away with trashing his pad and eating his grub, so it's time to put your dukes up and take the big fella down a peg or two.

3. You go out looking to fight a bear. Kudos to you.

Preparation

In our first two scenarios, you weren't expecting to fight a bear, so there wasn't much you could do to prepare for it—aside from reading this article, of course. If you're fortunate enough to be in our third scenario, I would offer these tips for advance preparation:

1. Bring witnesses. If a dude claims to have battled a bear in the woods, but no one actually saw the scuffle, chances are that the dude is a straight-up liar. Don't be that dude.

2. Have a drink. There's no sense in fighting a bear sober; you might lose your nerve. Think of whiskey as the lazy man's steroids.

3. Consider your wardrobe. Boots, jeans, and a t-shirt should suffice in a bear fight. Take off your glasses and put them someplace safe. Heavy leather gloves aren't a bad idea if you plan on grabbing the bear by its face, although teeth-mark cuts are probably the least of your concerns if it decides to close its mouth on your hand. Also, you don't have to dress like a GQ centerfold when you have your brush with destiny, so avoid accessories that could snag or be used against you by your opponent. Bonus points if you face the beast in the nude. No one will notice any temperature shrinkage when you're clobbering a bear with your fists; all they'll remember is how massive your package looked.

4. If possible, it couldn't hurt to get the bear drunk too.

The Brawl

Now to the meat of the matter: Actually fighting a bear. This is the point where you test your manhood and do away with any residual estrogen floating around inside your body. Good riddance.

A lot of so-called experts advise you to scare off the bear with loud noises and flailing. Intimidation is good, but you've got to start closing the distance between you and the bear before it runs off. Here's how:

First, establish eye contact. You need to lock in your opponent visually, establish your dominance, and challenge the bear's woodland authority. This is a great way to piss it off, which is necessary to provoke it into a fight. Scream in your manliest tenor, wave wildly, and be sure to flex your biceps a lot. Never underestimate the element of surprise and the impact of brazen masculine bravado. Having freaked out a bear, charge in no less than ten seconds, while the bear is still reeling from your display of testosterone—and the sheer size of your balls, if you happen to be in the nude.

If you're lucky, you'll land your first licks before the bear knows it's in a fight. Move quickly to bludgeon the eyes with hammer-like swings of your fist. Hitting any other place on the head is fruitless, due to their thick skulls. Don't just stand in front of the bear; keep moving. If you stand still, it's going to lunge forward and bring you down. Watch out for its front paws; it might try to sweep your legs out from under you.

Agility and smarts are your only advantage in a bear fight. After you've clocked the beast with your initial charge, cut sharply toward the bear. It is going to be spinning around to face you, so you're going to want to move with it, staying behind the shoulder to avoid its claws. You might be able to land a few one-handed shots to the bear's eyes while it tries to manage its own bulk. Inevitably though, the bear will stand. Once this happens, strategy is useless, and you have to play it by ear. That means knowing your opponent's capabilities and favored techniques.

Keep in mind that bears are natural wrestlers. They understand the basic principles of grappling and are physically equipped with a lot of tools that give them an advantage. Any bear that outweighs you is going to try to topple you as soon as possible. Instinctively, it will go for a crushing pin, then maul you with its powerful jaws. Don't let a bear gnaw on your skull if you can possibly avoid it.

If it rears up on its hind legs and lunges to push you down with its body weight, duck under one of its front legs and get to the bear's side. You might be able to sneak in a quick shot during this maneuver. Aim for the armpit. I got hit there once, and I almost cried. Almost.

A bear on all fours can also spring forward using its powerful hind legs while also swiping at you with its claws and gnashing with its mouth. Try to stay high, acknowledging that it would be better for it to snag your legs than your guts. If you're nimble enough, you can close distance with the bear and safely navigate into the crook of its neck. Once there, deliver elbow jabs to its eyes and any other soft tissue you can find to the rear of the jaw bone. Don't stay there too long though. You need to roll over that shoulder and get to the side of the bear again.

I know this is going to seem obvious, but anytime the bear tries to stand, you need to do your best to get in close and hit it as hard as you can in the groin. There's nothing worse than a shot to the danglies. I think it works on lady-bears too, although I'm not entirely sure.

It's tempting to try to mount the bear and rain down blows from above, but unless the fight is going so well that you can afford to score style points, I'd stay out of any position that allows the bear to control your body. It's important to remember that bears aren't afraid to roll over, and that would probably wreck your day. You'd be crushed, your insides would become your outsides, and the bear would look like it fell asleep in a cherry smoothie. Don't be a smoothie.

Never punch the bear's face straight on. That's a good way to lose a hand, and you're going to need both of them for the ridiculous number of high-fives later, if you emerge victorious. Also, fingers are a good way to keep track of how many beers you don't remember consuming when some pencil-necked bureaucrat tries to take you to court for being a man by assaulting a bear.

Since you're not likely to knock a bear out, and your hands are too small to choke it unconscious, you'll have to tire it out. Fighting a bear is a war of attrition. When that bear finally does slink off into the woods teary-eyed and cupping its groin, you can take solace in the fact that you'll never have to buy another round at Hooters again.

If you do somehow manage to kill a bear in hand-to-hand combat, drop me a line, because I'd like to buy you a beer. Of course, if it was a sun bear, you'll have to negotiate for a pink martini and a pat on the bottom. And by "negotiate," I mean arm-wrestle.

For legal purposes, this article does not condone the fighting of bears, regardless of how freakin' cool it is.

#2: BE A SUPERHERO

By Greg Kemp

The statistics are frightening: One in three people will be the victim of a violent crime at some point in their life. The police are overmatched, public money is stretched thin, and politicians don't care. Every man should do his part to rid the world of crime. Want to help? Become a superhero.

First off, don't douse yourself in nuclear fuel, or get expensive gene-altering surgery with the hopes of gaining real superpowers. It's not going to work, and you don't need superpowers to be a superhero. Batman is a master at vanquishing villains, and he doesn't have superhuman abilities. He just has big balls and lots of cash. You're going to do the same thing, with big balls only.

Step 1: The Litmus Test for Superheroing

Think you've got the cojones to be a superhero? Answer this: What does your sphincter do at the thought of facing down a carjacker who's armed with an assault rifle? If your sphincter so much as twitched, your best bet is to get active in a neighborhood-watch group. For those who revel in the idea of looking down the barrel of a gun and shouting, "Evil-doer, I rid the world of thee!" read on.

Step 2: Pick a Super-Theme

The super-theme is the foundation upon which your entire legend is built. Batman's signature is bats; Spidey's trademark is spiders;

Superman's calling card is steel. It doesn't matter what you pick—animal, mineral, bodily function—it's got to have an element of danger, and it's got to fit your persona. Remember, this theme is going to encompass every aspect of your superhero life, so search for something that mirrors and magnifies your own inherent kick-ass qualities. For starters, animal themes are a safe bet. Are you powerfully built? Consider the rhino or bull. If you're hairy, a bear might be a good choice. If animals aren't your thing, another possibility is to base your theme on a type of natural disaster, like hurricanes, earthquakes, or twisters. Any hazardous material can easily serve as a theme, from asbestos to diesel fuel. Think about all items that you have ever used that could be wielded as weapons for crime fighting, such as chainsaws or hatchets. If you happen to know Kung Fu, go with that.

Step 3: Turn Your Theme into a Kick-Ass Name

The formula to create a formidable name is simple: Amp up your super-theme with a few frightening words, military titles, or the letters Z, X, or Q. For example, "Captain Chainsaw," "Dr. Diesel," "The Asbestos Blaster," and "Hurricane Force Z" all sound powerful enough to do serious damage.

Step 4: Get a Supersuit

Supersuits hide your personal identity, protect your mortal flesh, and increase your mystique. Enlist a skilled tailor and remain anonymous. Polycarbonates are great for chest plates and helmets, but custom fabrication is not cheap. Don't pinch pennies here. Kevlar is the bread and butter of today's superhero costumes, but it'll cost you. You might be tempted by some of the new microfibers that breathe better than Kevlar, but be warned: They don't offer the same level of protection. Sweaty armpits are generally easier to deal with than bullet slugs in your aorta. Finally, be creative. You need to look the part. If you're Croc-Man, consider genuine crocodile skin with a Kevlar underlining. Sew croc teeth along the hem of the shoulders, to give your suit that extra bite of toughness.

Step 5: Weapons

Style is important. If you are the Aussie Wonder, wielding a boomerang completes the image. Are you an exterminator by day, Rat King by night? Fashion a rat tail that doubles as a whip. If you work as a pool cleaner, and you've selected a persona such as the Chlorine Catastrophe, get yourself a pressure sprayer and load it up with industrial-grade chlorine. Remember, if you lack skill with a respectable weapon, or can't pilfer stuff from your day job, consider taking out a loan and harnessing the power of modern technology. There's nothing wrong with using tasers to take down criminals, especially if you're the Electric Eel. Frequently, you can save money by using aftermarket equipment. Find great deals on exotic weaponry at foreign military-surplus auctions. There are still Saturday-morning weapons bazaars in most of the Balkan states, but make sure to get there early.

Step 6: Training

Being a superhero requires discipline. Cut back beer consumption to a case per week. Visit the gym daily. If possible, head to a secluded ranch in Montana, where you can master the use of your selected weaponry without arousing the suspicion of Big Brother. Most importantly, always remember to stretch first. A pulled groin can set you back months.

Step 7: Spread the Word

Pave your way with a good dose of PR. The best way is to get help from your local newspaper. Try to get a job as a reporter. That way, you can give yourself plenty of good coverage from the inside. If you can't get a job at a media outlet, try to hook up with a female reporter. If she's hungry enough, she'll do anything for a story. Alternatively, the articles will practically write themselves if the local media starts to suspect that you have a secret identity. If all else fails, put a classified ad in the paper akin to the following: *"Wanted: Criminals of all types. No prior evil-doing experience necessary! Meet me behind the 7-11 on Route 1. Signed, Captain Gonna-Whip-Your-Ass."* Your first few match-ups are likely to be entry-level criminals just trying to break into the field. Here's where you can really show off your skills.

Step 8: Taking Down the Evil-Doers

Superheroes do not simply round up bad guys and deliver them to the police. Superheroes prowl the streets to catch bad guys in the act, kick the shit out of them, and vanish into the night. When confronting an evil-doer, the element of surprise is your best ally. In time, as more men accept this noble call, order will be restored to the streets, and women and children will become safe again. But in no case shall you gloat about your achievements or use them to get chicks. Remember, the life of the superhero is a lonely journey. As Uncle Ben told Peter Parker, "With great power comes great responsibility."

Wait, forget that last bit. Using your superhero prowess to get laid or score free beer is a perfectly manly thing to do. In fact, you get extra points for wearing the supersuit in a romp.

#3: BUILD A FIRE WITH TWO STICKS AND A DIRTY GYM SOCK

#4: BREW BEER IN YOUR BASEMENT

#5: KICK ASS AT BLACKJACK

By William Tiernan

You know that guy your buddy invites to poker night who needs an explanation of the rules for every game you play? Or that guy who asks to join your group on the golf course, only to confuse "skins" with NFL football? Or that guy holding up the line at the sports book because he thinks "+3" means UNC is playing with three more guys than Duke?

Don't be that guy.

In order to participate in tons of typical guy activities, from poker night to golf wagering to the sports book at the Mandalay Bay in Las Vegas, every respectable man should have a comprehensive knowledge of all things gambling. To that end, what follows is a primer on how to play blackjack, also known as "21." Blackjack is played at one of the most sacred man-gatherings—the Vegas bachelor-party weekend—so you need to know what you're doing. The last person you want to be is that guy squinting at that blackjack crib card they give tourists, trying to decide whether to hit or stay with 14 against the dealer's five, as the rest of the people at the table pray for you to buzz off and try your luck at the Wheel of Fortune slot machines.

The Basics

If you play blackjack—in Vegas or anywhere else—you're probably going to lose money. You can use all the basic strategy you want and still drop a grand in ten minutes. Forgot those guys from Ben Mezrich's *Bringing Down the House* (the basis for the movie *21*); they were freaks from MIT who could recite the prime numbers from one to 1,000 in eleven seconds. Still, using solid basic strategy (with a touch of assertiveness) may lessen your financial blow. If you're lucky and smart, you may actually leave the casino with some real cash—which you can proudly blow later that evening at Sirens at Treasure Island.

Here's the cardinal rule of blackjack: What the dealer has is more important than what you have. Let me say that again: What the dealer has is more important that what you have. If the dealer shows six, five, four, or three, you will stay when your cards add up to twelve or more. Period. If the dealer shows two, you will stay when your cards add up to thirteen or more. If the dealer has two and you're at twelve, trust your gut. If the dealer shows seven or higher, hit until your cards equal or exceed what the dealer would have if he or she had a hidden face card. For example, if your cards add to sixteen and the dealer shows seven, hit. If you don't, leave the table, order a strawberry daiquiri, get a manicure, and go play in the kiddie station at Circus Circus. Having said this, remember: Unless you're the second coming of Rain Man, you don't hit once you've reached eighteen or higher.

Splitting and Doubling Down

Always split aces and eights, no matter what the dealer has. As for doubling down, if you have a nine or higher and your total is at least one more than what the dealer shows, double down. For example, if you have a six and a four and the dealer shows two, three, four, five, six, seven, eight, or nine—double down.

Special Situation: Double Downs and Splits

These are the situations that separate the Johnny Chans from the Jackie Chans. Remember that what the dealer has determines everything. If he or she shows five and you have two threes, take a chance and split your threes, assuming the dealer will bust. You might get a seven to match one of your threes. In this case you can double down and triple your money. Or, if you have an ace and a six and the dealer has six, double down. You probably will get a face card for seventeen, or maybe even a small card to reach nineteen, twenty, or twenty-one. Pretty strong for a double down against the dealer's six.

Aces

Aces are worth one *or* eleven. Don't be fooled into thinking an ace and a six is a good hand when the dealer shows eight. It's not. You have to play on the assumption that the dealer's hole card is a face card. A real man wouldn't stick in this situation. Nor would he stick with an ace and a seven against a dealer's nine. You've got to suck it up in these cases and take a card. If it's not another ace, or a two or a three, you still get another chance on the next card to make your hand.

It's Not Always About the Money

Using solid blackjack strategy doesn't ensure winning money (you didn't go to Vegas to win money, did you?). But playing like a real man could endear you to the stunning redhead sitting to your left. Maybe she's lost eleven hands in a row—even though, from my experience, women tend to be better blackjack players than men. She's now down to her last $25 chip. If you can tell she's about to call it a night, slide her a few chips and ask if you can play a hand for her. A few seconds later, you've split her fours against the dealer's five, paired them with two sixes, doubled down twice, received two face cards, and won both hands for her after the dealer busted for a cool $100. She smiles as the dealer stacks green chips in front of her, other people at the table are cheering, and you won your hand as well. Maybe she now wants your advice on every hand. Naturally, she's in Vegas for a bachelorette party; she just broke up with her cheating boyfriend; her friends are at the *Cirque du Soleil* show; your friends are at Caesar's playing poker; and the cocktail waitress is on her way with two Jack and Cokes.

Final Notes

Your manly blackjack play is wasted if you shack up all night at the $5 table. The $5 table is a great place to learn, but it's a sure way to bleed cash; over the long haul, the house is going to win out. Not sure of your table's limit? If there is a wheelchair player to your right, a chain-smoking convalescent-home escapee to your left, and a midget dealer standing on a box, chances are you're playing with red and white chips and fifty-cent coins. If you've arrived here accidentally, and you're actually trying to make money, leave this table immediately and search for higher ground. Who knows? You may walk away with a few $100 chips to your credit. My advice would be to cash one in and get yourself a steak at Delmonico in the Venetian—and use the other one as a ball marker during your next round of golf.

BLACKJACK GLOSSARY

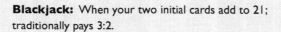

Blackjack: When your two initial cards add to 21; traditionally pays 3:2.

Shoe: A piece of equipment used to dispense cards; usually a plastic or wooden box.

Bust: When your cards exceed 21.

Push: When your hand equals the dealer's hand.

Hit: Taking another card; indicate a "hit" by flicking your fingers toward you.

Stand: Staying with the hand you have; indicate a "stand" by crossing your hand horizontally over your cards.

Double Down: After your two initial cards have been dealt, doubling your bet and taking just one more card.

Split: Turning one hand into two by dividing your two initial cards—which must be identical—while doubling your bet.

Surrender: Quitting the current hand while losing only half your bet; something that should never be done.

Insurance: Placing a second bet on the dealer to get 21 when he is showing an ace up; another highly discouraged move.

Face Cards: Jacks, queens, and kings.

"Monkey": Nickname for a face card; plead for a "monkey" after you've doubled down with a 10 or 11.

"Chicken Dinner!": Popular shout after the dealer busts; as in, now I have enough money to buy a chicken dinner. Sober or drunk, feel free to scream this, but only when the whole table wins.

"Color TV!": Same as "Chicken Dinner!"—only less common and funnier.

"Sir, please don't touch the cards": You placed your dirty paws on the cards again; this is a casino no-no.

"Sir, please watch your language": You dropped another F-bomb after losing your ninth hand in a row; again, another casino no-no.

Cash Advance: Using your credit card at 36% interest to get cash after you've gone bust.

Dear Mr. Man:

I'm throwing a bachelor party for my buddy, Flipper. We call him that because he can't swim. His fiancée, Julia, warned me there better not be any strippers, or she'll stick a taser to my family jewels. I want to be a cool best man, but I also want to avoid 10,000 volts in my scrotum. What should I do?

Signed,
Trying to Be a Good Best Man

Dear Trying:

Oh, I see. The "no stripping at the bachelor party" problem. I get this question all the time. Here's what you should do: Have the women show up naked.

Signed,
Mr. Man

#7: Win a Fight Quickly and Easily

By Alex Nowalk

ou're out-matched, out-numbered, or just plain unmotivated to get into a drawn-out scrape. No worries, this fight will be over soon.

The Headbutt

Take the element of surprise—and break his nose with it. A headbutt is simple enough to pull off. Lean back, arch your spine, and snap your head forward. You'll make contact with your opponent's face with the crown of your skull. Don't use your forehead—instead, try to connect higher up, around the hairline. This part of your head is extremely solid, and not all that sensitive. Try imagining his face as a soccer ball. For extra leverage, grab his shirt and pull him towards you, as you snap your head forward in one lights-out movement.*

The Throat Jab

This technique is not advisable unless the situation is life-threatening, as it takes only about 10 pounds of pressure to crush someone's wind pipe. In jail, you'll take far worse things than a beating. But, if the situation arises, one solid jab to the throat should drop any enemy.

* Disclaimer: I, in fact, headbutted a guy in a bar fight once. The next day I couldn't get out of bed. I think I may have herniated a disc.

Use the side of your hand like a karate chop. Get your opponent talking first, as he's more likely to lift his chin, exposing his throat.

Don't let him see it coming. In one swift motion, raise your right hand from your waist and snap it in a backhand motion against his throat. Your opponent should collapse immediately and begin to cough as he struggles to breathe. If he deserved a shot to the throat, go all the way and end his night with a knee to the face. If it helps you sleep better, he'll probably breathe a little easier when unconscious.

The Lazy Octopus

Slowly wave your arms about, as if floating in water or dancing on LSD; bend at the knees for extra dance-like effect. Try not to blink or break eye contact with your opponent. When he asks what the hell you're doing, answer matter-of-factly that you're an octopus. When he turns to his friends to confirm your insane antics, kick him squarely in the balls and run the other way. This technique can be modified with any odd behavior or interpretive dance.

#8: Defeat an Army of Ninjas

#9: Catch Fish with Your Bare Hands

#10: Deliver a Baby in an Elevator

#11: Capture a Sasquatch

#12: Throw a Perfect Spiral

#13: Grow a Successful Beard

By Brian Thompson

The beard goes by many names, from "face fungus" to "chin chinchilla" (and no, I did not just make that up). By sporting a beard, a man is telling the world, "No, I don't mind looking like a half-shaved gorilla. And yes, my testosterone levels are higher than your average prepubescent boy who isn't a circus performer." But depending on the landscaping of his cheek thistles, a man might also be proclaiming, "Yes, I live in a rotted cabin in Montana. And no, I have no use for shampoo." To be successful, the beard must invoke in onlookers the essence of "man" rather than "manslaughter."

So how does one grow a successful beard? It's quite simple, really.

Step One: Initiation

Go through puberty. You may think this step is a given, since the changes of sexual maturity are hard-wired into your very cells. But there are several environmental factors that can stunt or even permanently retard your growth into a bearded adult. If you look around your bedroom and see action figures on display, or *Star Trek* DVDs stacked on a shelf, chances are good puberty will come late for you. If you look around your bedroom and see action figures still in their packages, or a stack of *Babylon 5* DVDs, chances are good puberty will pass you by completely.

Here's another test: Cup your hand to your mouth and shout for your mother. If an apple-cheeked older lady comes bouncing down the basement stairs with a tray of pre-sliced peanut-butter-and-jelly sandwiches, you might want to consider back-alley testosterone treatments. If a middle-aged woman with a golden tan and succulently mature curves comes traipsing down the veranda stairs, you're probably a gigolo. In which case, no beard required.

Step Two: Patience

Stick with it. It's not enough to wait until your chin, cheeks, and/or neck wattle are covered in a fine mist of prickly hairs. Scruff is not the same thing as a beard. Given their druthers, most men would prefer a real, full beard over scruff, if only to cut down on the itch factor. But after enjoying the lustful gazes of scruff-attracted women, a man sporting a near-beard might be tempted to switch his clippers to an impossibly low setting and maintain a permanent "I-just-hopped-off-an overnight-transatlantic-flight" look.

It's true that many women believe themselves to be physically attracted to anything between a five and twelve o'clock shadow, but this is as good a time as any to tell you that women don't always know what they want. George Michael shook his leather-clad backside through the turn of the '90s, looking like he rolled a glue stick on his face and threw a handful of iron filings at it. He became a sex symbol among women because his perfectly kempt unkemptness reminded them of how a man is supposed to look when he rolls out of their bed in the morning.

What they didn't realize is that keeping your facial hair at a permanent volume of sexy scruff requires a commitment of time and effort that isn't manly. The successful beard shouldn't say, "I work hard to look good," but, "looking good flows naturally from my facial follicles." Whether you look good or not is beside the point. These women have no shot with George Michael anyway, so to hell with them.

Step Three: Definition

You've let your beard grow out, and now your face is warm and furry. No bar mitzvah, nudie magazine stash, or bare-handed jackal hunt could be a more potent symbol of your manhood. There are many different types of beard—the Forked Fingerpointer, the Lion's Mane, the Rocket Racer, the Spirit of Judd Nelson. All of these can be successful beards, and you can find more information about their shapes and origins at your local public library.

But it's also important to know what isn't a beard. A goatee, for example, is not a beard. In fact, the goatee is often confused with the Van Dyke. A true goatee only includes hair growing from the point of the chin, a la a goat. A Van Dyke is a goatee plus a connected mustache and is not the same thing as a Dick Van Dyke, which is a goatee and mustache combo that sometimes trips over an ottoman. A pointed goatee with an accompanying unconnected mustache is called a Fu Manchu and should only be worn by racist stereotypes and Klingons.

To be a true, successful beard, the facial hair must run across the chin from sideburn to sideburn and include a connected mustache. Which brings us to step three. You must now decide what kind of man you want your beard to represent. Are you a man of brawn and sweat? You might enjoy a thick, muscular beard style like those of your favorite paper towel models. Are you a man of brains and decisiveness? Your beard should probably be trimmed and clipped to straight, no-nonsense edges like the beards of your favorite steamy TV doctors. The thoughtful intellectual should strive for the long, tapered beard of the wizard or wise man. Every inch of your beard should be like the rings of a tree—denoting the hours spent pouring through textbooks, riding the giant tortoises of the Galapagos, or saving Hobbits from some dangerous something or other.

Before you ask: No, Abe Lincoln's chin strap cannot be considered a true beard. However, Lincoln demonstrated his manliness by freeing the slaves, preserving the sanctity of the United States, and taking a bullet. No beard required.

Step Four: Maintenance

Like a fine automobile, a cloak of freshly killed bear's skin, or any other symbol of manliness, the successful beard requires routine maintenance. Upkeep and care are what separate perfectly respectable bearded men from bearded crazy men. Most importantly, you should always check your beard for large objects. You'd be amazed what can become trapped in your facial hair from simple daily use. Anything from chunks of food to autumn leaves to dirty old tennis balls can find their way into your beard. Usually a simple brush with your fingers can do the trick, but some objects—including Velcro wallets, for example—may become so entangled that they must be cut free. These extractions will most likely leave a sizable hole in your beard, but this isn't much of a handicap. Fill the hole with seasonal decorations such as glass Christmas ornaments or chocolate eggs, and you'll simply look ready for the holidays.

Animals and other pests are likely to find the warmth and darkness of your beard to be an attractive destination. While squirrels, voles, and most birds can be kept away by wearing a straw scarecrow on your shoulder at all times, tics, weevils, and flesh-eating bacteria are harder to deter. For this reason, you should consider investing in a steel and concrete bucket full of sulfuric acid. I keep mine under my bed, and once a week, my beard starts its morning with a nice, cool acid bath. It takes no more than forty-five minutes of soaking to kill most small pests, and the lingering after-burn will keep them away for days.

You definitely don't want your beard to reach a Ted Kaczynski level of dishevelment. Kaczynski, if you recall, was the infamous "Unabomber," a disgruntled college professor who took to the woods and mailed explosives to people he didn't like. His beard was, frankly, out of control. After he was taken into custody, police discovered all manner of objects in Kaczynski's beard—including a typewriter, rusty pipes, and a nearly complete collection of old *Highlights* magazines. Despite the fact that Kaczynski authored a manifesto, he was definitely no man. Although he possessed a beard, his beard was unsuccessful.

Beards through Time

Like bell-bottom pants, the Swatch, and bigamy, any style of beard that has fallen out of fashion will eventually drift right back in. This is why it's important to familiarize yourself with the successful beards of the ages. Here is just a small sample of the myriad historical beards from which you may draw inspiration.

The Hollywoodian

Popular during the 1930s and '40s, this beard was modeled after the styles worn by Hollywood's glamorous elite, who trimmed their sideburns down to an almost nonexistent length and donated their clippings for use in "itch capsules," which Allied soldiers used to drop down the backs of Nazi shirts.

The Verdi

This early nineteenth-century beard is named after Italian opera composer Giuseppe Verdi, who combated the unmanliness of his profession with the raw, masculine power of his cropped chin hair and flamboyant mustache.

The Garibaldi

This mid-eighteenth-century beard was popularized by another Italian Giuseppe: Revolutionary Giuseppe Garibaldi, who was known as the "Hero of the Two Worlds," in part because he was able to unite both the hairy and shaven through the sheer awesomeness of his beard.

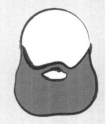

The da Vinci

This sixteenth-century facial fashion was invented by
Renaissance man Leonardo da Vinci on the same day
he invented the helicopter, the modern tank, the roller
derby, and the Ronco Electric Food Dehydrator™.

The Braided Fork

Eleventh-century Viking King Sweyn
Forkbeard had no choice but to grow a multi-pronged work
of art on his face or else sully the family name, though it
wasn't until his 12-year-old niece Gyerden suggested he
"pretty it up" with a few braids that this distinctive style
caught on.

The Zeus

The soft white curls of this ancient Greek beard were
the envy of mortal and immortal alike, though it wasn't
as widespread as it could have been, since Zeus—the
god of all gods—would often smite anyone he caught
"bogarting" his style.

#14: MAKE ASS-BANGIN' CHILI

By Alex Nowalk

If you don't like chili, get yourself examined. You may be a communist. With its rich history, bold flavor, and cornucopia of nutrients, who doesn't love chili? You can have it spicy or sweet. You can make it with beef, chicken, turkey, veggies, with or without beans—there's a variety of chili for everyone. My favorite? Any goddamn type that tastes good and has me cursing like a horny sailor the next morning on the toilet. See a man about a horse? Feels like the horse got liquefied, mixed with molten lava, and pumped directly into my colon. That's a meal you get to enjoy twice!

Ingredients:

Oil

1 large red onion, chopped (or 2 to 3 small yellow ones)

3 to 4 cloves of garlic, minced

1 pound of ground beef

3 peppers, diced (your choice; I use hot peppers)

1 to 2 cans of tomato sauce

1 can beans (I use red kidney beans)

Salt

Pepper

Chili powder

Cayenne pepper

Hot sauce

Bay leaves

Cilantro

2 beers

1 liter of Coca-Cola (This is for sweetness. If you don't like the idea of putting Coca-Cola in your chili, I suggest brown sugar or pancake syrup.)

These are your basic ingredients. You're probably wondering how much of each spice to use. Well, I can't tell you. The trick is to taste your chili every 20 minutes or so, and season as needed. Season generously, and don't skimp on the beer. It gives chili that extra smoothness. The crappier the beer, the better your chili will be.

1. Place a small amount of oil in the center of your cast-iron skillet over medium-low heat. Use just enough oil so it spreads as it heats.

2. Lightly sauté your aromatics (onion and garlic). Cook until onions have become soft and mostly transparent.

3. Break up your ground beef (or meat of choice) and cook until browned.

4. Drain the fat from the pan.

5. Add salt, pepper, chili powder, cayenne pepper, hot sauce (to taste) and stir; add half a beer and cook until most of the liquid is gone.

6. Transfer the contents of the skillet into a Dutch oven (or another large pot).

7. Add your cans of tomato sauce, peppers, bay leaves, cilantro, beans, other beer, and Coca-Cola. Leave the top off unless you're planning on cooking your chili for more than 12 hours.

8. Cook over medium-low heat until chili thickens and no sign of liquid remains when you stir. Taste every 20 minutes and season as needed.

Chili can be served solo, over rice or noodles, in a bread bowl—or simply serve it with a piece of your softest corn bread. My favorite way to eat chili is over a baked potato, skin on, with a dab of sour cream.

For spicy chili, accompany with a bottle of smooth, creamy beer. I prefer Killian's Irish Red or Honey Brown. For sweeter chilis, try a thicker beer like Guinness.

Leftover chili is great on nachos or can be recycled the morning after for a cowboy omelet. Add some peppers and onions to your eggs, top with chili, and enjoy clean sinuses before you even leave for work.

In Praise of the Dutch Oven

When it comes to chili, the most regularly overlooked detail isn't an ingredient—it's the pot. Sure, you could make chili in any old pot you have around that you use for boiling pasta. But the best chili requires the best equipment, and for my money there's no better chili-cooker than a Dutch oven.

A Dutch oven is a cooking vessel made entirely of cast iron, lid included. It heats evenly and, when properly seasoned, can add a subtle but exceptional touch of flavor.

Cast iron absorbs flavors, mostly from foods with high-fat contents, so the more you use cast-iron cookware, the better your food will taste. You'll also notice that the more it's used, the darker the Dutch oven will become. A well-used piece of cast-iron should display a glossy black sheen.

To prevent food from sticking, and to ensure that unique flavor, every cast-iron vessel needs to be seasoned. That means cooking fat or lard in the cookware to create a barrier that conducts heat from the metal to your food without charring or burning.

Seasoning your Dutch oven:

1. Heat your oven to 300 degrees.

2. Place bacon fat or lard in your vessel and put in oven for 15 minutes.

3. Swirl or brush the melted fat so it coats the entire internal cooking surface. Dump out excess fat.

4. Return to oven for two hours.

5. Repeat as needed.

A new cast-iron pan should be seasoned three or four times to create a solid foundational barrier. If rust or light spots appear in the pan's normal high sheen at any point, it should be re-seasoned.

THE LIFE OF CHILI

1510: Aztec Indians butcher a goat and cook its meat with *chile* pods. Chili is born.

1533: Aztecs butcher a conquistador and cook his meat with chile pods. Over a bowl of Chili, the first historically-verified account of a man saying, "tastes like chicken" is recorded.

1844: Chili moves to Texas with dreams of appearing in motion pictures, but ends up working with cowboys after being accused of creating eproctophilia. (Look it up.)

1845: After a particularly heavy night of drinking and eating Chili, grumpy Texans convince the USA to annex their state from Mexico.

1852: A man from New Jersey is the first person to put beans in his Chili. In reaction, Texas vows to execute more people than any other state. Later, Ghandi uses this same tactic, but replaces executing people with non-violent protest.

1934: Despite being in high demand, Chili feels slighted over being the second most popular food behind Soup. The two have never been seen at a meal together since.

1943: Chili is taken to Europe and helps defeat the Nazis. Some reports claim Hitler shot himself upon hearing the news that Chili had crossed the Rhine.

1965: Bob Dempsey marries his high-school sweetheart and lives for a year on his new wife's delicious Chili. Two months later they divorce, and Bob dies of a broken colon. He holds the record for longest amount of time lived eating only Chili, except for an unverified claim by a Siberian nun.

1974: The Feminist Movement picks Chili as their Man of the Year. He declines to attend the award ceremony because nobody likes a chick with hairy legs.

2008: Chili is eaten in every corner of the world, in hundreds of varieties. Many of those varieties include beans, so Texas keeps on truckin'.

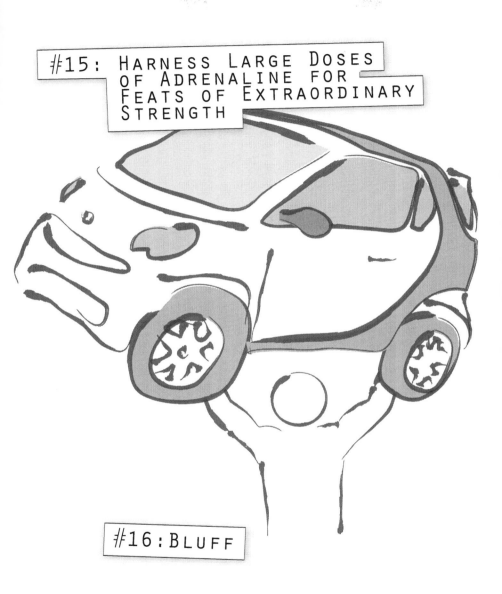

#15: Harness Large Doses of Adrenaline for Feats of Extraordinary Strength

#16: Bluff

#17: Cook a Steak

by Andrew Gori

If you want restaurant-quality steak but don't feel like putting your pants on, or are trying to convert some vegans, look no further. This is by far the easiest way to cook a juicy steak without reverting to wussy marinades or steak sauces. You'll need the following:

Steak

Canola oil

Kosher salt

Fresh-ground pepper

Cast-iron pan

Cooling rack

Aluminum foil

Tongs

Plate

Fork

Knife

Fan

Beer (lager would be nice)

An open window

1. Real men eat rib-eye steaks streaked with plenty of fat. The fat adds flavor and keeps the meat from drying out while it cooks. I've used London broils and New York strip steaks, but rib-eye is definitely the Rolls Royce of cuts.

2. Once you've got your meat, turn on the oven. I mean, right now. Go to your oven and set it to 500 degrees. Make sure the rack is positioned close to the top of the oven, because cooking these suckers quickly at high temperature is essential.

3. Place a medium-size cast-iron pan onto the biggest burner you've got, and set it to high. You can use any pan that's capable of sitting in a 500-degree oven, but the only pan a guy really needs is cast iron. It's perfect for camping trips—and also for bludgeoning intruders.

4. Lightly coat each side of your steak with canola oil. Be careful not to overdo it, as too much will make for a greasy steak. Sprinkle each side with kosher salt and fresh ground pepper.

5. Now wash your hands you filthy, filthy pig.

6. Open the nearest window and direct the fan—if you have one—to blow the air out.

7. When the pan is hot, drop the steak in for thirty seconds (I told you it'd be smoky). Use the tongs to flip the steak and cook it for another thirty seconds. Don't use a knife or anything that might pierce the steak because you want to keep the juices locked inside.

8. Place the pan—with the steak still in it, of course—on the top rack of the stove. Cook for about two minutes, flip the steak, and cook for another two minutes. This will give you a juicy medium rare, but if you're a big idiot and like medium, tack on another minute or two in the oven per side.

9. Remove the pan from the oven and place the steak on a cooling rack. Since I am too manly to own a cooling rack, I just remove one of the racks from my toaster oven and stick it over a plate. Once the steak is on the rack, loosely drape some aluminum foil over it.

10. Now get a beer out of the fridge and drink it at a moderate pace—say, two minutes. Your steak needs to cool, and the only effective way to stop you from digging in right away is the promise of a beer (again, lager would be nice).

11. If you're by yourself, feel free to eat in any fashion. If you're dining with others, you may want to consider putting the steak on a plate and cutting it with a knife and fork first.

12. If you add any steak sauce, I won't like you anymore—and neither will God.

That should do it. If you're fortunate enough to be cooking for someone other than yourself, do each steak separately. It'll ensure that they cook properly, and you'll get to drink more beers.

#18: RIDE A CHEETAH

#19: SMOKE A CIGAR

By Bryan Bechard

Before joining the ranks of cigar smokers, one must know the first rule of engagement: A cigar should never be considered a giant cigarette. One is an artful experience; the other is an addiction. Unlike the average cigarette smoker on break, a cigar smoker leisurely kicks back on his porch, fires up a handmade Montecristo, and sips a 12-year-old scotch. Million-dollar deals and world treaties have been sealed with cigars. In short, cigar smokers have arrived; cigarette smokers are just getting by.

Like wine, cigars are available in a wide range of flavors and quality. In the same way that Ripple cannot possibly compare to Dom Perignon, a Cuban puts grocery store Swisher Sweets to shame. The fun part is learning to tell the difference. First, though, the basics: You don't need to know a ton about cigars to be able to enjoy one, but failure to select, light, and smoke a cigar properly can serve as grounds for a return to the minor leagues of manliness.

Choosing the Cigar

Most smokers define a cigar's character by two primary components: body and flavor. Body refers to the strength and/ or intensity of the smoke; flavor is the taste that characterizes a particular cigar. A full-bodied cigar is perceived as strong, but does not necessarily suggest a lot of flavor. The two measures are entirely independent variables. Many veteran smokers favor cigars characterized by both full body and flavor. However, while it is generally accepted that one's choice of body—full, medium, or light—is a matter of personal preference, many assume that full-flavored cigars are universally considered the best, which is not so. Just as some individuals are turned off by full-flavored cuisine such as spicy Thai food, while others ravenously seek it out, some smokers prefer cigars that are more gently flavored. To choose a personal favorite, let your palate decide.

Body and flavor are determined by three cigar elements: (1) the filler tobacco in the center, (2) a binder leaf that holds the filler together, and (3) the outer wrapper, which is rolled around the binder. The source of the cigar and the type of seeds from which it is grown determine the taste and thickness of the smoke. Generally, the lighter the wrapper, the lighter the smoke. Cigars from Jamaica are usually considered mild. Dominican Republic offerings vary from mild to medium in strength. Honduras and Nicaragua tend to be stronger and heavier smokes. The ever-coveted Cubans are considered some of the richest and creamiest cigars in the world.

Don't be afraid to experiment with different cigars until you discover a personal favorite. It's all a matter of taste. Indeed, even your own tastes may change as you embark on a lifelong relationship with cigars. The same type you initially consider a wonderfully robust smoke may leave you wondering if the manufacturer has altered the blend years later as your tastes evolve.

Cigars are meant to be stored in an environment between 65°F and 70°F, with a constant humidity at approximately 70 percent, never to exceed 72 percent. If conditions are not ideal, the cigar can become too wet or too dry and affect its overall quality.

The dimensions of a cigar are measured in ring size and length. "Ring gauge" specifies the diameter of a cigar, and is based on 64ths of an inch. Therefore, a cigar with a 32 ring gauge has a diameter of a half-inch, and a 48 ring gauge is three-quarters of an inch around. Length is expressed in inches.

There are a range of names for standard cigar sizes, including Rothschilds (4 ½" x 50), Robusto (4 ⅞" x 50), Julieta, also known as Churchill (7" x 47), named for Sir Winston Churchill, Prominente/Double Corona (7 ⅝" x 49), and Presidente (8" x 50). Figuring out your favorites through experimentation can be fun, but if you're just starting out, go to a reputable cigar shop and ask for some initial guidance. In general, $8 to $10 will buy you a decent cigar. A slightly larger investment of $10 to $20 should get you a superior one.

Cutting the Cigar

Cigars are held together at the closed end by an edible flavorless gum. In order to smoke the cigar, you need to get past that "cap," which means cutting off just enough of it to create a comfortable draw, but not so much that the cigar unravels. To cut the cap, use a cigar cutter. The edges of your cutter should be sharp enough to slice through the cigar without ripping or tearing it. Single-blade cutters are available at any smoke shop and are cheap enough to be treated as disposables and can be replaced when they become dull. There are many types of cutters available, but it is nearly impossible to go wrong with a single- or double-blade model.

To make the cut, look toward the cap end of the cigar for the "shoulder," the accepted name for the bulge. Place the cutter's blade at the start of the shoulder, and push your fingers together in a single snap-like motion. This will give a nice wide mouth from which to smoke. To ensure that the hole is large enough, do a "cold taste" by taking a small draw off the unlit cigar. If the airflow is poor, snip a little more from the end.

Lighting the Cigar

Opinion is split about whether the paper ring near the cap should be removed before or after lighting a cigar. Leaving it in place lessens the chance of damaging the cigar by removing it. However, there are a fair number of smokers who collect the paper rings—like baseball cards, as a matter of personal pride—in which case, removal is best to do before you light up. If you're a beginner, it is wisest to leave the ring alone. It's one less piece to worry about.

There are two acceptable tools with which to light a cigar: (1) butane lighters or (2) cigar matches. Both use clean, odorless fuel, so that the flavor of the smoke is not affected. Do not use candles, cigarette lighters, or paper matches. These items release chemicals when they burn, which noticeably affects taste.

Light your cigar by holding it away from your mouth, just above the flame. Then toast it like a marshmallow, rotating it in your fingers until the entire edge starts to cook. Go slowly. After 15 to 20 seconds, remove it from the flame and blow on the lit end to see if there are any spots that need further heating. Put the cigar back above the flame for another 10 seconds or so, then take a draw on it, to ensure that it is fully lit. A few draws should give you a nice red-cherry ring at the end, which is a good sign.

Once lit, unfinished cigars should never be mixed with fresh ones. Storing previously lit cigars with unlit ones fouls the taste of the entire batch. Far worse, an attempt to store lit cigars with unlit ones can quite easily cause your entire cigar collection to go up in smoke.

Smoking the Cigar

To maximize the experience, pour yourself a drink to keep your palate continually cleansed. Anything from water to brandy will do. As you smoke, a certain portion of tobacco may end up in your mouth. Spitting is acceptable—as long as you are outdoors, of course.

First-time smokers occasionally get into trouble by trying to smoke a cigar like a cigarette, by drawing the smoke into their lungs. Seasoned cigar smokers tend to draw only into their mouths, which takes a fair amount of time and repetition to master. To practice the mouth draw, inhale without the cigar and hold your breath. Then drop your jaw to pull in your cheeks. This creates the vacuum critical to the mouth draw. Some smokers prefer the full lung draw, but to ensure that your experience does not turn into a sudden coughing fit, take small draws and exhale them somewhat quickly. More experienced smokers hold the smoke in their mouths for a few seconds before exhaling, to savor the body and flavor of the cigar.

Holding the Cigar

There are two basic methods to holding a cigar: (1) between your middle and index fingers, like a cigarette, or (2) between your thumb and first finger. The method you choose is a matter of preference and personal style, but in either case, the cigar should be rotated every minute or so to keep it from *canoeing,* or burning unevenly. If it starts to canoe but you catch it early, rotate the unburned section so it faces upward. Heat naturally rises, which means the top side should burn faster to correct it. If you find yourself in a full-blown canoe, relight the cigar or try to remove the non-burning side while ashing.

Ashing the Cigar

A well-rolled cigar can burn slowly and create a stiff ash up to two to three inches in length before it needs to be tapped off. Ash maintains the same general consistency and appearance of the rest of the cigar, except for a distinctive grey hue. Should your ash break up quickly, or if the ash color begins to vary, the smoking characteristics of the cigar are probably below par.

If you're outside, gently tap the end of your stogie just past where the ash ends on a hard surface with a corner or edge, such as a chair arm. You can also use your thumb to tap the mouth end of the cigar when using the two-finger grip. With the finger-to-thumb grip, tap the top of the cigar, Groucho Marks-style.

Ashtrays are a critical component of the smoking experience. Your ashtray needs to be large enough to handle the ashes from two full cigars. Otherwise, the mountain of ash constantly needs to be shifted or emptied frequently. Proper ashtrays have a divot—known as a "rest"—on at least one side, to hold the cigar and prevent it from rolling to the side. When smoking with a companion, you need an ashtray with two rests and an even larger size to hold the ashes, to savor the experience without interruption.

Finishing the Cigar

A quality cigar can usually be smoked down to the nub, way past the band. If you did not remove the ring when you first lit up, you'll need to do so before you reach the end of your cigar, so it doesn't catch fire. As the cherry gets closer to your mouth with every draw, the smoke becomes thicker, and it may be necessary to open your mouth slightly to intake air with your smoke. This technique thins out the cigar, cooling it so that it can be enjoyed longer. Sometimes during the process of smoking, the taste may change from smooth to bitter, or have a distinct aftertaste. This may be due to an irregularity in the tobacco, known as a "tar spot." Often, the cigar can burn itself past a tar spot if you put it in the ashtray for a minute or two.

Typically, a good cigar maintains its slow-burning qualities from three to five minutes without being puffed. Continue enjoying your cigar until the smoke gets too hot for taste, or the cherry gets too close to your fingers. Never extinguish your cigar out by stubbing the end into an ashtray. Proper etiquette calls for you to let it die out naturally. Pointing it down will end its life quickly, resulting in less of a lingering odor and residue. Finally, above all, remember: Cigars are meant to be savored. Save the cigarettes for the 10-minute smoke break.

#20: PLAY BEER PONG LIKE A PRO

By Tahra Seplowin

Perhaps it's the cheering spectators, the free-for-all taunting, or the fact that beer chugging is an integral part of the competition. Or maybe it's simply the double entendre of getting your balls into as many cups as possible. Whatever the attraction, beer pong is a time-honored sport—yes, it is a sport, with official national championships—played in dorm rooms, backyards, and casinos across America. If you haven't played, it's time to rip the door off its hinges and prop it up on some extra chairs.

The Basics

Beer pong is a mix of basketball, ping-pong, and the good old-fashioned art of getting wasted. In some circles, beer pong is also known as "Beirut." Some insist that beer pong is played with paddles, while Beirut is not. Others say the opposite is true. Still others consider the two terms interchangeable; these players may or may not consider the use of paddles sacrilege. If you just want to get drunk and play ball, you'll probably want to avoid the "beer-pong-versus-Beirut" debate.

In most cases, beer pong is played as a two-person team game contested on a waist-high table top the length of a standard door. Players attempt to get a ping-pong ball into a cup in their opponent's triangular 10-cup formation. Two beers are distributed evenly among the 10 cups, so that each is approximately a quarter to a third full. (Plastic ribbed cups are preferred for easy measurement.) When you make a shot, one of your opponents must drink the beer in that cup, and then discard the cup. The first team to hit—or "clear"—all 10 cups wins.

Picking a Partner

Picking a good beer-pong partner is a little like choosing a presidential running mate; you need someone who complements your strengths, compensates for your weaknesses, and serves as an "attack dog" when necessary. Study the list of beer-pong "personalities" before your next game; picking the right partner could be the difference between being the last man standing and the first man to vomit in the trashcan.

Playing the Game

The official rules of beer pong are that there are no official rules. Got that? Good.

Still, there are some general guidelines that govern most beer-pong events—at least for the first few hours, before players start lobbing ping-pong balls at each other instead of the cups. If you're new to the game, familiarize yourself with these basics.

1. Each team gets two shots per turn. If a ball is scored in your cup, start chugging. Depending on the house rules, failure to drink immediately may result in an "extra cup" penalty; or, if the other team throws the second ball into the cup you should be drinking from, it may result in an automatic forfeit. When the beer is gone, toss the cup.

2. The ping-pong ball will visit the floor, so each team should have a "dunking" cup of clean water. No one wants to swallow lint, dirt, or pubic hair—typical of a frat house—with their beer.

3. As cups get cleared, you may be allowed to rearrange them, but house rules vary. You may get one "re-rack" per game, or you may be able to shuffle cups only after a certain number are gone. If it's permitted, experiment with different strategies for the re-rack. Some expert beer-pong players like to arrange all their cups in a straight vertical line. Others prefer the steadily diminishing pyramid.

4. The first team to clear the other team's cups has almost won. Tipping the table in a drunken stupor to achieve this goal does not count. If that team went first to open the game, the second team gets its "fair ups." If they manage to clear the rest of the almost-winner's cups without missing once, the game is declared a tie. Set up the cups, pour the beer, and play again.

5. Approved throwing techniques include the bounce, with a single hop of the ball into the cup, ideal for players with miserable aim, with the exception of games in which house rules allow for bounces to be swatted away; the arc, or a basketball-style jump

PLAYER	PROS	CONS	GRADE
MR. HIGH TOLER-ANCE	Can handle much of the drinking responsibilities; shot accuracy improves with alcohol consumption, which makes him an asset late in the evening when you're singing "Shock the Monkey" at the top of your lungs.	May lose on purpose so he can drink more.	A-
MR. GOOD ARM	Shoots about 90% from the field.	Can't have it all—accuracy falters as consumption increases.	B-

shot; the fastball, guided by the principle that the shortest distance between two points is a straight line, especially when you're drunk; the "cocky," in which the player shoots with eyes closed, off the wall, over the shoulder, or some other flashy method.

6. Keep your Zamboni handy. A towel, rag, or sweatshirt should be kept close to sweep spilled beer from the table.

7. When is it over? A beer pong event is over when: A) you run out of beer or ping pong balls; B) someone breaks the playing surface; or C) more people are surrounding the toilet than the beer pong table.

PLAYER	PROS	CONS	GRADE
MR. INSULTER	Hurls a fresh mix of insulting, hilarious, and ridiculous insults at the other team; his wit and enthusiasm can distract opponents, which is key because like other sports, beer pong is a game of inches.	Starts fights.	B+
Ms. Never Played Before	If she teams up with you, she may like you; inexperience may cost you several games, but you might "score" later.	Spotty shooting and drinking.	B
Ms. Definitely Played Before	May distract opponents with brash confidence; can hurl insults and beer-pong balls with the best of them; high tolerance. Guys generally don't expect women to beat them, thus the perfect secret weapon.	After people see how good she is, you're going to have to go against every he-male that wants to be known as the one who beat "That Girl."	A

Dear Mr. Man:

When I party, I like to show off my breasts. I especially like it when my female friends look at them. It's a real turn-on for me. But it makes my boyfriend uncomfortable. So here's the question: If everyone likes to look at my breasts, and I like to show them, why is it considered socially unacceptable?

Signed,
Love to Show My Tits

Dear Love to Show My Tits,

I don't know. Will you marry me?

Signed,
Mr. Man

#22: Open a Beer Bottle with your Teeth

#23: Let your Dad Win an Argument

#24: RESCUE CHIVALRY

By Alex Nowalk

I f every girl wants to be a princess, then every boy wants to be the knight who gets to carry her off into the sunset. Yet the world has changed drastically since the feudal system gave birth to such gallant, albeit rigid, dichotomies. Some things don't change, though. People need help and protection, and sometimes these people are women. There are still people who endanger others; they need to be stopped. So how do you apply chivalry in a modern world? We can't all mount up and trot through downtown looking for someone to joust.

Allow me to illustrate with an example from my personal history: Once, while enjoying a cigarette outside a bar, I witnessed a redhead struggling to get to her car. She was supporting her plastered date and being heckled by a group of four or five college-age guys. They made lewd comments about her skirt and told her to ditch the guy in favor of spending the night with someone who could "still get it up." One of them even began walking after her as she strained to make it to her car.

Perhaps I should have stepped in at that point. I could have had words with the guy, been all chivalrous and gallant. All I had to do was climb into the saddle and charge. I didn't.

Instead, I waited—and watched. When the girl came back, welcomed by a second round of jeers and cat-calls, I asked her if she wanted me to say something to them. She laughed, waved them off, and thanked me. After retrieving her purse, she drove off.

I didn't have to take a beating, and the girl got home safely. Does my failure to intervene physically make me a coward? Is her honor tarnished because of my non-action? I don't know much about honor—even less about courage. While many people lament the death of chivalry, I prefer to think that chivalry has grown up, not vanished. It's about time we rethought the rules of chivalry, and updated them for the twenty-first century.

Rule 1: Avoid unnecessary violence. Unlike knights, you shouldn't be looking for a fight. When conflicts occur that can't be talked out reasonably, wait for them to blow over, or leave. Use your body to impose a presence between people if the situation reaches a boiling point. Aggression on your part will only add fuel to the fire.

Rule 2: When in doubt, ask. If chivalry aims to protect honor, let her determine if her honor has been offended. There's a good chance whatever offense you're eagerly waiting to right has already rolled off her shoulders. If it doesn't bother her, it shouldn't bother you. Ask if she needs help, and if she does, intervene with words before you take a short-cut to fisticuffs.

Rule 3: Wait until she's safely away. Whether she's given you the green-light or made it clear she can handle it herself, hang around until you're sure the conflict has been resolved or until she's clear of the scene. Most situations can be diffused with a few cool-headed comments and a few minutes of stalling. Give her time to get into her car or somewhere more public, or flag down help if the situation is dire.

Rule 4: Don't make it about you. I'm sure I could've worsened the situation outside the bar by responding to the guys with insults, walking towards them, making eye contact and standing with my arms crossed, and daring them to become even more belligerent. Don't use chivalry as a cheap way to showcase your manhood. If you want to help, be sensible and help; don't be quick to act or get hot-headed, and don't jump into a fight.

Rule 5: Chivalry isn't a pick-up line. Yes, I know, the entire motivation behind wanting to be the knight on the white horse is to get the girl. Too bad. Read a book and have something to talk about if you want to pick up a lady. Don't offer your assistance and expect her to swoon or invite you back to her place for an all-night thank you. If you help, she'll be grateful—but not that grateful. If you happen to stumble along a beautiful woman who requires assistance, great. Don't go looking for one. Just because she has a uterus doesn't mean she can't handle herself. Also, don't assume only women can use a hand from time to time. If you want to be chivalrous, be color-, age-, race-, and gender-blind.

At the heart of chivalry is an idea: The strong should protect the weak. We can no longer define strength by physical prowess; we can no longer define weakness by anatomy. If you lament the death of chivalry, you are really mourning the death of a dream. Life is no fairytale. For those who have outgrown the fairytale but refuse to believe chivalry is dead, I applaud you. But if it is to survive—as more than a quaint relic of antiquated values—then we must all ask what we can do for the new chivalry, whether that means discovering strength that can't be developed in a gym, finding the gentleness to offer assistance without ulterior motives, or simply understanding that in some situations we are not needed.

SECTION II:

THE IMPRESSIVE MAN

How to Wow, Woo, and Be an All-Around Winner

#25: Lose Weight, Get Ripped, and be Sexy Like Me

By Steve Chang

I am not an active man. I don't do yoga. I don't do Pilates. I don't bench press my body weight with my head between another man's legs.

But I'll tell you what I *do*. Follow my plan, and you'll never spend another lonely night at home with your cat. You'll be sexy, like me.

Diet

1. Stop drinking beer.
Start drinking whiskey.

2. Stop eating dessert.
Start smoking cigarettes

3. Stop being so fat.
Seriously. Just don't eat so much.

Workout

First, you'll need to understand your musculature.

Human Musculature

Can you find your *latissimus dorsi*? Do you know what a *trapezius* does?

If you're reading this, the answer is probably no. The only exercise you do is the grievous toilet squat, and the occasional 40-ounce curl. Furthermore, I suspect you probably don't care.

Luckily, you don't really need to know all of the details. Just remember that all your muscles can be classified into one of two groups:

1. Pushing muscles

These are the muscles that push stuff away from you.

2. Pulling muscles

These are the muscles that pull stuff towards you.

Pushing muscles

You'll need two exercises to work this group:

1. The Push-Up

2. The Dip

Start with the push-up. Do it once. That's called a "rep." Now keep doing it until you have to stop. That's a "set." Do three sets of as many reps as it takes to make you cry.

Do the same thing with the dip.

Are you sore the next day? Good. You had a good workout. Not sore? Do more sets of more reps, you fat lazy goon.

Pulling Muscles

You'll need two exercises to work this group:

1. The Pull-Up

2. The Curl

As above, do three sets of each. Now admire yourself in the mirror.

Man! You look *pumped!*

Do pushing muscles one day, and pulling muscles the next. If you do both types of muscles in one day, you will die.

Lower Body

Your *legs?* Look, man...when you're cruising the parking lot of the mall in your totally wicked IROC-Z with a six-pack of Smirnoff Ice in the back, do you really think those girls can see your *legs?*

Abdominal muscles

You know how real men work their abs?

They have sex. They have lots of sex. And not just with themselves. If you're doing it right, that'll be all the workout you'll need.

Try My Program for One Month!

If you don't look better in a month, you're hopeless. Just give up. You'll be ugly forever, and nobody will pretend to like you unless you're rich.

#26: Score Two Tickets to the Daily Show

#27: Win a Chariot Race

#28: BE A CHEF IN THE BEDROOM

By Karen Gibson

 fore·play: \fôr-plā\

    1 : erotic stimulation preceding sexual intercourse

    2 : action or behavior that precedes an event

It's a known fact that both men and women like foreplay. We just have different definitions of the word. *Merriam-Webster's Dictionary* gives a good global definition, but men and women were created differently, and therefore require unique approaches. For men, something as simple as an innuendo, a glance, a view of an apple-shaped bottom, or a bit of cleavage may be all it takes.

However, when it comes to preparing for *"a night of debauchery,"* *"that special time together,"* or whatever terminology floats your boat, women are like crock pots; they take some time to get warmed up. But as the heat deepens, the meat softens and the juices begin to flow. You reach the point where you can dip the ladle in and find manna from heaven. Men, on the other hand, are like microwave ovens: Ding! Dinner's ready!

If you're like most men, you probably think you learned everything you need to know about foreplay from *Playboy*. Just push, pull, and turn in concentric counter-clockwise circles. Warming up has nothing to do with it. But, gentlemen, take it from a lady: To bring out the tiger in your sex kitten, foreplay must begin outside the bedroom.

Step 1: Fill the crock pot with all the important ingredients for a delicious meal later tonight.

Start first thing in the morning by telling your special lady how good she looks. Brush her hair back from her neck and lightly kiss her exposed nape. Then say, "Have a great day. I'll see you tonight." Unless you're already known as the romantic type, trust me, you'll pique her interest.

Step 2: Plug in the crock pot and set the desired cooking temperature.

Sometime during the day, give her a call and let her know that you are thinking about her. Tell her you miss her, and you're looking forward to some time alone tonight. Use phrases such as, "I want to be able to take my time making love to you," or "I just can't seem to get you out of my mind. I'm looking forward to touching you." If you're not used to getting sexy on the phone in the middle of your workday, push your boundaries a little. Imagine what your woman might want to hear. The pay-off? Now you've got her mind right where you want it.

Step 3: Check on the meal's progress and make adjustments as necessary.

When you both get home, check in with her. Give her a long, "God, I've missed you!" Kiss her, ask how her day was, and listen to her answers. Ask questions to uncover any hidden obstacles to getting her in the mood. Do the kids need tending to? Are her shoulders and neck locked up with tension? What can you do to help make sure she's relaxed and energized when the time comes? You wanna play ball? Help prep the field!

Step 4: Serve the long-prepared meal on attractive plates.

Any good chef will tell you that presentation is vital in showcasing an exemplary dish. So shower, shave, and tend to yourself. Draw your lady love a bubble bath, so she can soak and relax while you take care of any last-minute tasks like getting the kids ready for bed. When you finally make it to the bedroom, start off with a whole-body massage to ease her tense muscles. Light a few candles. Create ambiance with music, lighting, and a warm, inviting bed.

Step 5: Take your time and enjoy the meal you've taken so long to prepare.

After all this work, who wants to rush? Start with lots of kissing—everywhere. If you've been together for years, show her how well you know the combination to her safe. Your slow enjoyment shows her how much you desire her. Nothing turns a woman on like feeling wanted.

If you take the time to follow these steps, you'll be sure to get things cooking. Not every "meal" needs to be a big production, but knowing what's on the menu ahead of time whets the appetite! Bon appétit!

#29: BEHAVE AT THE GYM

By Jeff Bender

Maybe it's the lights catching the gleam of our greased shoulders, the windows displaying our pecs to the outside world, or the mirrors presenting that dimple in our calves at its linear best. Maybe it's the girls—running, biking, or otherwise circling the gym's perimeter. Whatever the reason, we're compelled to feel as though we're onstage at the gym, as though every fellow patron is watching us—at least in her periphery—and admiring the hell out of our tris.

But pan away for a second. How many of the other patrons do *you* watch? Do you behold the ball of someone else's bicep as it flexes? Do you run on the treadmill, all the while tracking a certain leg lifter's struggle through his workout? Do you cross your legs in silent awe of that stud who's *killing* the recumbent bike?

The answer is no, you don't—and neither does anyone else.

If the gym is like a stage, it's a pathetic one at best. People don't pay to see your bare arms any more than they pay to feel the room jolt as you slam your dumbbells to the floor after a set of incline bench. Slamming weights is never necessary, by the way. Let's be honest: If we're strong enough to pick them up, we're strong enough to set them down.

So here are five tips for your next visit:

1. Cover up.

Wear a damn t-shirt to the gym, not a leotard. Since nobody's watching, you don't have to humiliate yourself by putting "the guns" on display. Wearing a sleeveless number of any sort goes against both self-respect and fashion. Plus it makes you look effeminate. I don't mean gay; I mean effeminate. Wear a white, gray, or black t-shirt to the gym; ditto the shorts. Wear sneakers and socks. Do not, for any reason, forego those last two—or those first two, for that matter.

2. Talk to someone.

Finally, you'll get some real perspective about the place where you work out. The gym doesn't have to be a lonely, headachy place. Ask someone to spot you on the bench; then offer to spot him (or her) on the next set. Afterward, introduce yourself and move on to the next exercise. You'll get out of your own head for a second, and quit scowling at these people who are trying to do exactly the same thing you're attempting to do. Plus, you'll now have someone to spot you. When in doubt, it never hurts to have someone watching over you.

3. Lose the flair.

Going to the gym does not make you an athlete. Real athletes work out six days a week, often twice a day. Their workouts are far more various and intense than yours, and on game day, they subject themselves to risk of injury, failure, and public humiliation on a scale you'll never totally understand. So, let's be clear: you're a gym-goer, not an athlete. Nobody's showing up to watch you, and you're not saving the world by upping the leg press another ten pounds.

4. Breathe, don't grunt.

Another act of performative narcissism: grunting. Ideally, the gym should sound like a Lamaze class, not an endless series of Serena Williams tennis serves. Grunting expends energy that you need to complete your rep, and blocks oxygen from getting to your muscles. Breathe instead: out on the press, in on the release.

5. Don't admire yourself.

Which is to say, after a set of dumbbells, don't nudge up to the mirror and lift your sleeve to show the dimpled, precarious result. It happens maybe more than you think. Track the next guy you see coming off a set of tricep pull-downs. Follow his triumphant gait past the mirrors to the water fountain and then back to the rack. You'll see what I mean.

To be fair, it is easy to get caught up in the mirrors, lights, and music of the gym—just as it's easy to forget that you're not starring in some glamorous sports movie. But a film about a sleeveless guy who runs the treadmill at seven miles per hour and falls asleep, intermittently, on the leg press? Come on. A little humility goes a long way in this paranoiac room we call the gym.

#30: Get in Touch with Your Inner Child

By Padraig Carty

To get in touch with your inner child:

Have manners that are meek and mild.

Don't hog the telly for the football game,

Watch something suitable for a dame.

Show your feelings, and learn to cry.

Why, even learn to bake a pie.

As for the whole domain of fashion,

You've somehow got to find a passion.

Read romantic novels by the score,

Then ask your dear one to lend you more.

There's no better way to show you love her

Than being patient with her mother.

If forced to choose twixt shopping and baseball,

Say to your girl: "Darling, it's your call."

But beware, oh beware—for if you follow my advice,

It will soon be the girls who are throwing the dice.

#31: Hold your Girlfriend's Purse while she's in the Dressing Room

#32: Perform Open Heart Surgery with a Corkscrew and a Spoon

#33: Clip your Nose Hair

Dear Mr. Man:

I'm having trouble with women. I think it has to do with my drinking. When I'm on a date, I like to order a refreshing glass of cold milk. But my dates always end early. My question: Is there something wrong with drinking milk?

Signed,
Milk Lover

Dear Milk Lover,

I like milk, too, especially with cookies or doughnuts. But drinking milk in public is destructive to a man's image. Many women unfairly characterize milk drinkers as weirdoes. My cousin is convinced milk drinkers are perverts. While there are no scientific studies linking milk-drinking to anything except thirst, it's generally a bad practice for a man to be seen drinking milk in public. So don't do it. Not at restaurants, strip clubs, or your son's little league ball game.

Don't despair. There are a few instances where a man can drink milk.

1. Next to an open refrigerator, straight from a gallon jug. If you are seen, say you just ate five jalapeno peppers and there wasn't any Colt 45 to wash it down.

2. You are paid an obscene amount of money to do it. For example: A buddy offers you a thousand bucks to suck milk straight from a goat's teat (you should probably be drunk for this stunt).

3. It's Christmas Eve, and you're Santa Claus.

Hope this helps, Milk Lover! Best of luck with the ladies!

Signed,
Mr. Man

#35: MAKE A BEST-MAN SPEECH

By Bobby Nelson

Being named someone's best man is an incredible honor. Of the three billion guys on earth, your buddy chose you to stand next to him at the altar. However, once you get past the initial novelty of the request, being asked to be a best man quickly begins to feel more like a monumental burden. First, you have to let some tailor get perilously close to your pills when he's measuring you for a tux. Then, you're trusted with a solid-gold symbol of love that screams "pawn me" after your bookie has called for the seventh time. You have to throw a bachelor party that makes the groom forget he's headed to the gallows. You have to scout a stripper for the bachelor party (this should actually be a fun thing, but I digress). Perhaps worst of all, instead of getting drunk at the reception's open bar like all of your friends, you have to make a speech in front of everyone the bride and groom has ever cared about.

You're on your own with the grabby tailor and the stripper, but with my help you'll give a brilliant oration that wins over the crowd, leaves sentimental guests reaching for the Kleenex, and inspires a few moms to introduce you to their single daughters.

Make Your Buddy Look Good

There's a reason your buddy put gel in his hair today and donned a suit that fits: he wants to look as classy as possible. Don't ruin all his hard work by telling everyone about the time he crapped himself while hitting on the dog at his twenty-first birthday party.

There's a good chance your buddy isn't a saint. Who is? So, how can you give a touching, honest, and entertaining speech without resorting to stories that will make Grandma write him out of the will? Feel free to talk about tough times, as long as there's a happy ending. Maybe your parents' divorce was messier than Courtney Love on a bender, and your buddy got you through it. Maybe you helped him overcome his unhealthy addiction to *World of Warcraft*. A Cinderella story of obstacles overcome will bring everyone in the room into a circle of camaraderie with you and the groom.

Tell a Story

Everyone likes a good story. If someone says they don't, they're a damn liar, and you shouldn't feel bad about drinking their glass of champagne when they go to the bathroom. Solid story themes include: the first time you guys hung out; the last time you hung out (excluding the bachelor party); the day he first introduced you to his bride; and the day he told you he was engaged. If the groom is your brother, offer a story from your younger days, or a story that highlights your maturing relationship. Keep it short and relatively obscure. That way, if it flat-lines, you may be able to salvage some laughs or tears with an improvised detail that no one but your buddy will be able to disprove.

Acknowledge the Bride

I don't care if she's a succubus sent here to steal your buddy's soul. Her dad is paying for the food and liquor you're enjoying, so suck it up and be nice. Plus, she's willing to take a chance on your buddy for the rest of her life—how bad could she be? If you acknowledge the bride in a positive manner, maybe she'll extend the groom's curfew the next time he hangs out with you. Try providing some jocular advice on how to "handle" your friend. Keep it simple: "Wifey, I know you'll have an incredible time being hitched to this guy. Just make sure you don't leave him alone with a plate of brownies."

Inside Jokes Are a No-No

It may be pants-pissing hilarious, but if you and the groom are the only ones laughing, be ready for a long evening. The point of your speech is to ensure that your buddy is loved and appreciated by everyone in the room, not just you. Anything that requires a "you had to be there" caveat belongs in your high-school yearbook, not your best-man speech.

Improvise

This isn't a fifth-grade book report, so don't make it too scripted. If something funny or endearing happens between the chapel and the recital hall, bring it up. For instance: "Ladies and gentlemen, I don't know if you saw this, but when leaving the wedding chapel, Don Juan here actually had a pair of slippers waiting for Wifey in the car, so she didn't have to walk around in heels for the rest of the day." Pause for the "awwww" and turn to your friend. "Is that what you want to do, buddy? Make the rest of us men look bad? This speech just turned into a roast." If your rehearsed speech is going over well with the crowd, embellish and extend. There's no reason not to give a few extra jabs to your buddy if everyone is laughing along the way.

Note that successful improvising means knowing your audience. This is tricky enough, but consider the fact that you have to cater to people ages five to 99, and you've got yourself a ball-twisting social conundrum. A good rule: stick to gentle gender stereotypes (like the presumption that women love shopping; men love sports) and simple humor, with jokes that can be understood by second graders and senior citizens alike.

Sneak in Something Heartfelt

The best-man speech is the one time you get to say something quasi-emotional about your friend without being mocked mercilessly for being a pansy. This section of your speech should be crafted to make him look like someone capable of caring not only for his friends, but for the woman to whom he just pledged his life. As an added bonus, you stand to score some sensitivity points with the bridesmaids. If you wish to retain your masculinity while you're pledging affection, try this classic move: "You know, we never say this because we're guys, but—I love you, man. Now, in order to retain some masculinity, let's arm-wrestle."

Do Not Bring Up the Wedding Night

You know it. They know it. Everyone in the room knows it. They're going to have sex. We get it. Unless you want to be thrown out by the bride's father, or join the Bad Cliché Hall of Fame, I suggest you stay away from this topic. The bride may withhold sex from your buddy that night just to spite you and your loud mouth. Good luck getting your shit back from his house after that one.

You may think these pointers will make for a long-winded best-man speech that takes up valuable drinking, cake-cutting, and funky-chicken-dancing time, but you should be able to get it done in five to 10 minutes. If you use my tips and fit them to your style (as well as your buddy's situation), you'll pull off an entertaining best-man speech—and improve your chances of securing some "post-wedding entertainment" of your own. Cheers!

#36: Understand the Four Cs of Diamond-Buying

#37: Date an Identical Twin

#38: Control Space and Time

#39: KNOW FOURTEEN WAYS TO A WOMAN'S HEART

By Teresa Sultzbach

1. Tools: Power tools are your friends. So is your woman's vibrator. Do not be intimidated if she knows more about both than you do.

2. Tongue: Speak more than one language. Sports lingo does not qualify as a second language.

3. Laundry: Do not underestimate the sexiness of a man who can speak eloquently about Tide versis All. Show me a man who can sort, wash, fold, and put away clothes properly and I will show you a man who gets laid *all the time.*

4. Barber: Trim that hair. Hint: we're not talking about facial hair. Trimming your nether regions is highly recommended, since we ladies don't like hair in our teeth either. Hairy backs are a no-no; if we want to see Darwin's missing link in action, we'll visit the Museum of Natural History.

5. Autos: There is something undeniably sexy about a man who knows his way around an engine. Maybe it's the attention to detail, or maybe it's a great ass bent over the hood of a car. Whatever the appeal, a man who knows cars seems as though he might not mind spending a little extra time under your, um, hood.

6. Mommies: We do not want to be your mother. Especially if we are busy mothering our own actual children. We want an equal

partnership. We understand that the balance of who does more is likely to shift from day to day. As long as the responsibility is accompanied by appreciation, we are happy to do things for you. We hate to nag, really. We do like to take care of you, just not all the time. We also like to have sex with you. If this reminds you of your mother, I can recommend a great book. It's got this guy named Oedipus in it.

7. Masseur: Know how to give a massage, and give them for more than just foreplay. A massage is one of the most singly unselfish acts that a person can do for another. Granted, massage can lead to great sex. Knowing that your partner is doing something solely for your benefit can be a turn-on. We just might feel like reciprocating.

8. Kids: First and foremost, you do not "babysit" your own children. I have heard countless dads say that they are babysitting their kids. Have you ever heard a woman spew this nonsense? Second, diaper changing is not the sole domain of mothers. There is not a female gene that makes cleaning up poop any more palatable to us than to a male. Thirdly, with older children, cereal and chicken fingers are not a food group. Know how to feed your kids healthy stuff.

9. Bugs: Killing bugs is a man's job. Period. We might even let you skip doing the dishes tonight, if you simply kill whatever is scurrying across the floor. We might be able to handle frogs, but killing a cockroach and picking up its squirming body is just too much.

10. Gifts: Pick your own. Your secretary is not sleeping with your wife. She wasn't there when your sweetie rested her head on your shoulder and said she wanted to be with you for the rest of her life; she wasn't there when you watched your darling walk the aisle in white; and she wasn't there when your wife pushed something the size of a cantaloupe out of an opening the size of a kumquat. So why is she deciding what to get your wife? In theory, you

should know us better than anyone else. We appreciate almost anything you pick out for us, but stay away from appliances; unless we have specifically asked for a vacuum, don't bring home a Dyson, because that vacuum is likely to be the only one sucking anything in your house for weeks to come.

11. Directions: Why is it such a hardship for men to ask for directions? Are you scared of looking stupid in front of us? I guarantee that driving around lost for hours and refusing to ask for help makes you seem like a much bigger imbecile.

12. Tits: Know how to tell fake ones from real ones. What is the appeal of silicone boobs anyway? Imagine if men had the ability to augment themselves with silicone. Wouldn't the guy with the real 10-inch penis feel a little irritated about a fake cock stealing all the attention? We feel the same way when it comes to boobs.

13. Cooking/Food/Wine: Food is a very sensual thing in many ways. It involves all of your senses, from the presentation to the scent to the texture of the meal. A man who can cook or appreciates good wine is someone who enjoys engaging all their senses. That's a very good asset in bed.

14. Limitations: Every man has a talent. It could be dancing, it could be taxidermy, or it could be cooking. If you aren't good at something, don't pretend to be. If you can't dance or sing, a career on Broadway is probably out—and that's perfectly fine. Be confident in your abilities, but not blind to your limitations. Besides, I can't remember ever seeing a tap-dancing taxidermist on "Hell's Kitchen," can you?

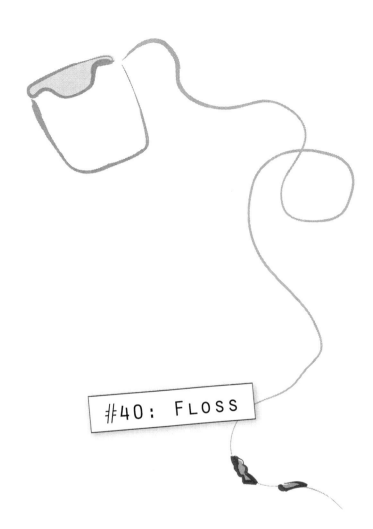

#40: FLOSS

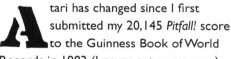

#41: Host (and Win) an Atari Tournament

By William Tiernan

Atari has changed since I first submitted my 20,145 *Pitfall!* score to the Guinness Book of World Records in 1983 (I never got a response). The company that started it all now produces games such as *Neverwinter Nights* and *The Witcher*. But new-age gaming is not for me—particularly after my six-year-old nephew beat me 6-0 twice in Wii *Tennis*. Call me old-school, but I prefer pre-1986 Atari, with the 2600 black and brown console system that accepts game cartridges both right-side-up and upside-down.

Rationale

It's Saturday, and you've run out of things to do with your buddies. Everyone is still recovering from that trip to Vegas, and the court where you play pick-up basketball is overrun with eight-year olds on skateboards. You could iron your clothes for the upcoming work week, or you could host an Atari tournament. Why Atari rather than PS3 or XBox? Because Atari is cooler, and the last time you played it with a group of friends you probably couldn't drink—unless you started boozing in fourth grade. Now you can take beer back in time, which might actually turn *Space Jockey* and *Home Run* into cool games.

You may think playing outdated video games is less manly than playing real sports. Never fear. An old-school Atari tournament is an incredibly manly activity. How do I know? First, the word "tournament" comes from the Old French word "torneiement," which refers to a medieval martial-arts contest featuring a bunch of knights—essentially dudes of yore–on horseback who tried to beat the crap out of each other. Second, I remember that WWF legend Hulk Hogan once said he liked Atari in a TV interview.

Preparation

Who still has an original Atari console? One with at least two joysticks *and* two paddle controllers, commonly referred to as "spinners"? I do—but if you don't, one of your buddies might. If not, you can snag one on eBay for 30 bucks. Ten games typically equate to the cost of one burrito. Next, you need a 15-inch Zenith television or something comparable; old-school Atari should be played on an old-school television to accommodate the crappy graphics as intended. Try your local Salvation Army thrift store, or just walk out to the curb on trash day. Finally, you need somewhere to play. The ideal place is the house where you played Atari as a kid. Hopefully, it's close to where you live now—but not so close that they're one in the same, especially if you're over 30. If your childhood home is within 20 miles or so, give your parents a pair of movie tickets and send them out for a few hours; playing in their house gives you home-field advantage.

Food, Drink, and Ambiance

An old-school Atari tournament is an '80s event. Do it right, with all of the proper accessories. Serve peanut-butter-and-jelly sandwiches on Wonder bread, plastic-wrapped cheese and crackers duos with that red plastic spreading stick, Hi-C, and beer. Make a glam-rock mix tape featuring Poison, Skid Row, and Cinderella. In keeping with the '80s theme, you may want to throw your R2D2 and Chewbacca action figures on top of the Zenith. Dig your John Riggins poster out of the closet, and paste it on the wall. Behold the sight of R2D2, falling off the TV when one of your buddies goes ape shit after pulling a 7-10 split in *Bowling*, while Riggins inspires you as you play *Superman*. Granted, you could go all out with the wardrobe by requiring Jams, but some things are best left to the '80s.

Competitors

You and four or five buddies.

Games

You're hosting, so play to your strengths. If you excel at blowing things up, go with *Asteroids, Space Invaders, Robot Tank, Defender, Combat,* and *Laserblast.* If you're peerless with the spinner, include *Breakout* and *KaBoom!* If you have quick hands and favor the joystick, make sure *Frogger, Pac-Man,* and *Missile Command* are in the mix. If you want to drink heavily, choose *Tic-Tac-Dough.*

Implement two house rules:

1) *E.T.* is forbidden. *E.T.*—as in, The Extra-Terrestrial—is the single worst game created by Atari. In fact, many link its release to the decline of Atari. According to the *Alamogordo Daily News*—later confirmed by *The New York Times*—in 1983, Atari dumped between 10 and 20 semi-trailer truckloads of its games into an El Paso landfill. It is suspected that a majority of those games were *E.T.*

2) Include at least one game that requires the spinner control; this ensures a well-rounded champion.

Side note: The game *Laserblast* advertised that something monumental would happen when a player reached 1,000,000 points. Well, I have a friend whose brother tried. He played for six straight hours—his mom spoon-fed him lunch and dinner—and when he finally reached 1,000,000, a series of tiny exclamation points scrolled across the screen:

!!

He responded by putting his foot through the Magnovox (tip: shoes should be required when playing *Laserblast*).

Winning Tips

1. There's always one joystick that works better than the other. Mark the "preferred stick" and insist on using it during head-to-head competition. As host, you have this right. You can't put a beat-down on your buddy in *Hockey* if you can't get your slap shot off.

2. The tournament should last at least two hours, so cover the top half of your joystick with felt wrap to prevent blistering.

3. Be sure to invite at least one new-age gamer, and one guy who grew up playing ColecoVision, Atari's competing system; it takes these poor bastards at least an hour to acclimate.

Special Regulations

1. Anyone who knocks Chewbacca off the television must shotgun a beer.

2. Anyone who throws a beer can at Riggins is immediately disqualified from competition.

3. Anyone who scores over 20,000 in *Pitfall* gets to sit in the La-Z-Boy for the remainder of the tournament.

Format

Host your tournament in a round-robin format. Each player faces off against three other players in a best-of-three match-up. As tournament director, you should post all matches on a huge piece of posterboard, with corresponding start times and games. A victory equals one point. After the "regular season," the two players with the most points square off in the finals. The finals represent a best-of-seven series, with players alternately selecting the game to be played. The finals should include at least one game of *Combat*—because it's so bad, it's fun—and one game of *Bowling,* which requires no skill. The finalists may very well be loaded by this point in the tournament. The players who sucked too bad to make the finals must retire to a different room to eat the remaining peanut-butter-and-jelly sandwiches and watch *Ernest Goes to Camp.*

1st Place Prize

Dig up one of those ribbons you won back when you were eight years old for the Fourth of July egg toss, and affix the appropriate name—hopefully, yours—and date with the title: "Atari Master of the Universe." If one of your buddies has passed out by this point, go ahead and pin the ribbon to his nipple until he wakes up.

#42: ASK HER TO MARRY YOU

By Eden Anthony-Black

The movies make it look so simple: Buy a ring, get down on one knee, use four little words, and have a hankie ready. Piece of cake, right?

I'm sorry to say that in the real world, proposing to the woman of your dreams is not always so easy. Take it from a woman who has experienced two of the world's worst proposals (see the *Don't* section below). There is a right way to propose and there is a decidedly wrong way.

Don't:

■ *Propose during or immediately following sex.* In all likelihood, your brain isn't functioning on all cylinders at this point. You might not remember it in the morning, but she will.

■ *Pop the question publicly.* It might seem romantic to put her face on the Jumbotron, or to take a knee during her family reunion, but by doing so, you are forcing a "yes." Unless she's got ice in her veins, she won't shoot you down in front of 50,000 Red Sox fans or her grandma—but she may not be so happy later.

■ *Hire someone to propose for you.* There are service companies that will send a yahoo in a gorilla-in-a-tux costume to your woman's office to do the deed for a nominal fee. No matter how madly she loves you, this approach deserves a no.

- *Ask her to spend the next 50 years with a green finger.* If your proposal is spur of the moment and all you can find is a $20 ring from a casino gift shop, don't wait longer than a week to replace it with the real deal.

Do:

Be creative.

- Is her favorite sitcom being made into a movie? Arrange for a private screening and have the theatre show your proposal in lieu of previews.

- Is she a fan of musicals? Tie the ring to a single rose a la *Phantom of the Opera* and leave it on her pillow. Does she get misty-eyed when she listens to "Bless the Broken Road" by Rascall Flatts? If so, write her a letter about how your life was crap until you met her—and read it to her before you propose.

Do your homework.

- Listen to her comments about items in the latest jewelry catalog. Some women are allergic to gold; others hate diamonds.

- If she reads marriage-proposal stories out loud to you—a sure sign that she's ready for you to pop the question—watch and listen. Does a specific part make her tear up or catch her breath? Incorporate relevant details into your proposal.

- "Borrow" one of her rings. (Make sure it fits the right finger!) Bring it to your jeweler for sizing.

- The next time you're strolling through the mall together, pop into a few jewelry stores to browse the merchandise. Take note of what sizes, styles, and colors she likes. If she models a ring that makes her face light up, but your jeweler doesn't carry the same one, draw it out for them. They may know a goldsmith who can re-create it.

- Mean it. If her best friend's man proposed at the Christmas party, and she has told you the story 16 times, it doesn't mean you have to ask her to marry you on New Year's Eve. Propose when you're ready, using your own style.

#43: Apply for a Patent

#44: Make your Mother Proud

#45: KNOW A FEW $5 WORDS

By Alex Nowalk

As a man, you may find yourself in situations where you'll need to impress people with more than just body hair, beer, or a loud grunt. Sad, but true. For those rare occasions, every man needs an intimidating vocabulary to fall back on. Whether you want to impress your boss, confuse the aggressive ape at the end of the bar, or catch the ear (and eye) of a pretty lady, try dropping any of these word-bombs.

Loquacious [adjective]: excessively wordy or long-winded. As in: "With a few drinks in him, the man slipped into a loquacious tangent." [la-kway-shiss]

Jeremiad [noun]: (generally) a long, mournful complaint; (specifically) a lengthy literary work that bemoans the state of society and morality. As in: "Tim's wife is a feminist, and by that, I mean if you talk about sports, politics, or anything else with her, she goes off on one of her man-hating jeremiads about female empowerment and domestic serfdom." [jer-uh-may-ud]

Katzenjammer [noun]: (literally) the shrieks and lamentations of cats; (figuratively) 1) a din of various noises; 2) an exceptionally unpleasant hangover. As in: "During Octoberfest, most tourists in Germany experience a katzenjammer upon waking." [kats-en-jam-ur]

Defenestrate [verb]: to throw someone out a window. As in: "When his girlfriend threw him out of a second-story window, Steve became the first person in our town to be defenestrated." [dee-fen-eh-strate]

Ontological [adjective]: concerning or related to the field of philosophy (ontology) that deals with arguments of being, existence, and the nature of reality. As in: "Melissa's belief in evil gnomes is not an ontological statement, but a combination of too much reefer and childhood trauma involving a family of midgets." [ont-oh-loj-gik-al]

Triptych [noun]: a work of art in three pieces or sections. As in: "The three new movies make six *Star Wars* in all, ending the trilogy debate and securing *The Godfather* as the best cinematic triptych ever." [trip-tick]

Consubstantial [adjective]: composed of the same essence or material, specifically, regarding Catholic theology and the triad of Father, Son and Holy Ghost. As in: "After dropping out of seminary, Nick was known to frequent a local pub and console distraught women with the promise that we're all consubstantial in the dark." [kon-sub-stan-shaul]

Antediluvian [adjective]: (generally) something very old, outdated; (specifically) something from the time before the Genesis flood. As in: "Your maternal ancestor's antediluvian lifespan dates back to the founders of Babylonia. Yeah, your momma is freakin' ancient." [an-tee-duh-lue-vee-ahn]

Facetious [adjective]: lacking serious intent; amusing; frivolous; not to be taken literally. As in: "The narrator's use of hyperbole and stereotypes made it obvious his statement about the immorality of killing hookers was facetious." [fah-see-shiss]

Eproctophilia [verb]: being aroused by or engaging in sexual activity involving flatulence. The fact that you want to see how to use this word makes me think you'll figure it out. [ee-prokt-o-fill-ee-ah]

#46: Give up your Seat on the Bus for Pregnant Women, People with Disabilities, the Elderly, and Brazilian Supermodels

#47: PLAN A ROMANTIC VACATION

By Dorothy Carlow

Your girlfriend just graduated from medical school. Your fiancé is totally stressed out about the upcoming wedding. Your wife has been dropping hints about the dream vacation you've never taken her on in the 10 years you've been married. Whatever the occasion may be, there is *never* a bad time for you to plan a surprise vacation for the woman in your life.

Simple and Fun: The Weekend Away

You will need: an overnight babysitter if children are involved (which means that it may be time to cash in that favor with grandma); cleaning supplies; a reservation at a nice hotel or bed and breakfast; plans involving something your lady loves to do.

1. The trip should be planned around the activity. Yoga, kayaking, the theater...whatever it is that she loves, take her to a place where she can experience her favorite activity in an authentic environment. If she loves rock climbing, don't take her to the big hill down the street—get to the mountains, where she can really test her ability. As for accommodations, pick something clean and classy, but not wallet-busting. The hotel or bed and breakfast should be part of the experience, but not the whole thing.

2. Pack her bag for her. Include clothes she likes to wear. No, you won't get it perfect, but do your best, and include things she might

need for her special activity. If you've booked a yoga session, make sure you pack her mat; if it's rock climbing, get the right shoes. Then, when she's up and ready to start another boring Saturday, tell her you've got an idea. Grab her packed bag from the closet, ask her if there's anything she needs for the night, and off you go.

3. Know where you are going, bring directions, and don't make her drive.

4. Bring some snacks and drinks for the car ride.

5. Drive straight to her activity. Get her oriented, make sure she has what she needs, and leave her to it. No, you don't need to do it with her; it's not couples yoga time. The activity should be paid for in advance (as in, before you leave for the weekend). For massages, this includes the tip.

6. While she's doing her thing, don't drive to the local watering hole. Instead, head to the hotel or bed and breakfast, check in, and inspect the room! Make sure it smells and feels fresh, and add a few signature touches, such as champagne or flowers.

7. Pick up your lady at her activity. Ask her how it went, and bask as she gushes about what a great a time she had. Don't let it bother you if she got a message from a guy with the same name as you. This stuff happens.

8. Keep dinner simple. If she wants to go out to eat, take her to the local favorite. Make sure you have researched your options ahead of time.

9. Don't get too invested in elaborate after-dark fantasies. You're probably going to get some, but if you don't, don't worry. A stellar weekend pays off in the long run, like when your lady drops NFL playoff tickets on you. A football game lasts at least three hours. That's better than something that might last only five minutes. Right?

Expensive and Exotic: The Loooooong Vacation

You will need: a credit card and lots of cash, vacation days, a travel website or agent, an extended babysitter (if necessary), and strong organizational skills.

1. She's been talking for years about her perfect vacation, and it's not five nights in Vegas. Figure out when both you and she can take days off, line up child care (possibly bribing mom into coming to play grandma for the week), and book the trip. Yes, she'll know you're going somewhere, but there can still be an element of surprise. Don't tell her where you're going. Guys have trouble listening, so she won't expect you to remember her ideal vacation. She'll be thrilled and surprised when you pull it off.

2. Choose a hotel, not a house. A rental house might look good online, but it might have mold, mice, and leaky plumbing. Hotels are more likely to have spas, activity planners, good restaurants, and clean towels.

3. Plan activities. You don't need to fill every hour of every day, but plan a few relevant activities. For example, if you're doing a

"tropical" vacation, book a snorkeling trip, a boating excursion, and surfing lessons.

4. Surprise, surprise! Don't give it away, no matter what.

5. Purchase travel insurance, in case of hurricanes or other natural or unnatural disasters (e.g., your airline goes out of business).

6. If you're in line for a promotion at work, ask for it. If not, go for it anyway. This trip is not going to be cheap—but you only live once!

7. As the vacation draws near, drop a few destination hints, so she can pack accordingly. You don't want her packing bikinis if you're going skiing in Colorado. Yes, she should pack for the long vacation herself; she simply can't afford to spend a week-long trip with the wrong bras.

8. It may be a long flight. You don't have to fly first-class, but you should bring her favorite snacks and food on board. She'll appreciate the thought and the fact that you won't have to spend ten bucks for a bag of Doritos and a Diet Pepsi. Also, provide in-flight entertainment; if she loves cards, have a deck ready for some Crazy Eights. And bring some of her favorite magazines.

9. Spend money where it counts. Know what's important to your lady, and don't skimp on those things. Does she care about cars? Make sure you rent something classy. Does she love a comfy bed and a huge bathtub? Spring for a top-notch hotel room.

10. Bring cash; it opens doors, especially in foreign countries.

11. Don't take her on any timeshare presentations that offer a $50 gift certificate to Red Lobster (generally avoid locales that have Red Lobsters). This type of behavior is cheap, not to mention a waste of time. These presentations usually last about two hours, you'll get harassed by the salespeople, and even worse, you might end up buying 1/26 of a piece of property you've never seen before!

12. Again, the exotic vacation is not all about sex. If you plan it right, there's going to be plenty in store for you. The bigger reward exists down the road when she returns the favor. It might be a flat-screen for the basement, a new videogame system, or a $500 gift card to Hooters. Well, maybe not Hooters…but membership into the club of "Guys Who Plan Kick-Ass Romantic Vacations" definitely has its privileges.

Free and Fantastic: The Stay-Cation

If you're completely strapped for time or cash, don't despair. You can take your lady on a romantic vacation tonight, without leaving your home. You will need: a bathtub, bubble bath potions, rose petals, candles, cleaning supplies, an Egyptian cotton bathrobe, soft slippers, scones, tea, and wine.

1. Make sure the tub is spotless and fill it with hot water.

2. Add the rose petals and bubble bath potions.

3. Light the candles around the tub.

4. Tray the scones and tea.

5. Invite your loved one into the bathroom.

6. Give her a 30-minute foot massage while she soaks in the tub.

7. Provide her with anything else she wants for the next 30 minutes.

Note: If you're really feeling crazy, double up and break out the romantic bath treatment on the weekend trip or exotic vacation, to score even more points.

#48 : STONEWALL

#49: GET DRESSED (EVEN IF YOU LOOK GREAT NAKED)

by Alyssa J. White

Not many women will say it, so I must: Guys, most of you suck at getting dressed. A friend told me that her man once asked her, "Honey, do you like my outfit?" Instead of telling him the truth—that he looked like a clown—she said: "I like you better naked." She figured it was nicer for him to walk around with that in his head instead of *my girlfriend is embarrassed to be seen with me.*

A little brutal fashion honesty would go a long way for at least 70 percent of the male population. The other 30 percent are either: (1) gay (which is not to say that all gay men dress well—they just don't have embarrassed girlfriends), or (2) have sisters who let them know that their tie looks like the one Uncle Vern wore to Aunt Ethel's funeral last year. What follows is a simple set of head-to-toe guidelines—not rules—for the fashion betterment of that 70 percent.

Hats

I know you love your favorite hat and have since the eighth grade. Believe me, I want you to have things you love, but if it smells or is changing colors, save it for watching sports with the boys. Don't try to kiss a woman while you're wearing it. Two other basic guidelines:

1. Hats should not be worn in restaurants, in church, or at the dinner table.

2. Consider whether your lid fits your situation. For example, that adored baseball cap belongs on your head during the game only if your team is in the World Series. Berets are acceptable if you hold an elite military position, and bucket hats are okay to wear in the pool or on the beach. Please remember: Camouflage or fluorescent-orange hats are for hunting, and *only* hunting.

Hair

Be it short or long, treat your hair like you love it. As long as it's clean and well-kept, your girl will feel the same. If it's short, close trimming around the edges will keep you looking sharp; if long hair is your get it trimmed frequently to avoid split ends and promote a shiny, touchable look (which I can safely say that all women love). I'd also recommend a little gel or, for guys with curls, some mousse. Women touch; we just need a a little encouragement.

Shirts

Shirts deserve the most attention, but frequently get the least. When it comes to shirts, size matters. If you've got a nice set of pecs, women want to see them. If you're not a chiseled gym rat, that's okay, too. In either case, don't do the oversized shirt. The shoulder seams should fall on the outside edge of your shoulders, not on the middle of your biceps. The hem of the shirt should rest near your hips, not at mid-thigh. Keep in mind that if you're trying to hide something, we're only going to look harder for it.

The color and pattern of your shirt also makes a difference. As a general rule, stick to basic colors, and tread carefully with patterns. Patterns often mix colors that end up confusing even the most careful dressers. Also, it's extremely important to avoid wearing two patterns in the same outfit. You might be wearing an awesome striped button-down that fits you perfectly, but those plaid shorts your mom got you for your birthday will blow the whole look. When in doubt, follow this basic rule: if you're wearing a patterned shirt, go with solid pants, and vice versa. For those who want to take it to the next level, here are a few things to get you there:

1. Wife beaters
   or muscle tanks are for working out and mowing the lawn only. They are generally not the type of fashion statement you want to make.

2. Shiny or sequined shirts are just plain bad. They show every bit of fat you might have and make every bit of muscle look like fat. Trust me on this one.

3. Argyle and sweater vests are for golfing and other such country club activities exclusively.

4. Paisleys are scary. They look like flowery sperm drawings, and should never have been put on clothing in the first place.

5. Turtlenecks are for men over 30, very single, and interested in staying that way. By very single, I mean that they haven't dated in five years, and probably won't for the rest of their lives—especially if they keep wearing turtlenecks.

Jewelry

Although jewelry is a touchy subject with some men (and women), it's an easy call. If there is any doubt, skip the jewelry. If you must wear jewelry, try to match your accessories—gold with gold, silver with silver, etc. Please note that wearing your high-school class ring makes you look like you're stuck in the past. Get over it. Oversized gold chains just draw attention to unsightly chest hair. If a piece of jewelry doesn't make a positive statement about you, it's a distraction from the masterpiece.

Belts and Other Stuff

Wearing a brown belt? Resist the urge to put on black shoes. Don't mix and match, ever. Some men take this to the extreme and wear either black or brown all the time to avoid confusing the two in the same outfit. However, if you decide that you can handle having both colors in your closet, note the following:

1. Brown shoes and belts can be worn with khakis, greens, blues, and browns.

2. Black shoes and belts can be worn with khakis, blacks, grays, and blues.

3. As for wallets, nobody ever looks at them; they pay attention to what comes *out* of them.

Trousers

If you only take one piece of advice offered here, make it this one: Pleated khakis, or any other pleated pant for that matter, are out of the question. I don't care if you are walking out the door and spill a jelly donut and coffee on your best dress slacks. Those pleated pants are reserved for yard work. Changing into them is *not* an option. A few other pointers:

1. Be wary of cuffs and pants that are too short. The best way to deal with a flood is an ark.

2. Don't hike your pants up into your crotch so high that we can see the white socks you're wearing with your dress shoes.

3. Avoid Wrangler jeans unless you actually wrangle livestock.

4. For shorts, watch the length. Nobody really wants to see above your knee. If they do, it'll probably involve taking the shorts off completely.

Socks

Match the color to the shoe. Wearing white (or brightly colored) socks with dress shoes is simply unacceptable. White socks can be worn with sneakers, period.

Shoes

Shoes that don't lace are the trickiest. Cowboy boots are fine if you're line dancing, live in Texas, or wear Wranglers (see livestock precondition above). Clogs or other no-tie shoes (excluding sandals) should only be worn with pants long enough to cover most of the area where the laces should be. This will eliminate the dreaded "duck" look.

Crocs and guys? Tough call. If you feel strongly about it, go for it. Although they are durable, comfortable, and great for rafting or loafing around the yard, I personally do not consider Crocs a positive fashion statement. Warning: opinions vary widely on this issue. Tread at your own risk—literally.

While on the subject of shoes and feet in general, would it kill you to trim your toenails? When we see you wearing bright-white tube socks with your Birkenstocks, we know what you're hiding.

Be Yourself

Don't wear anything that you can't wear with confidence. No woman has anything against a man with his own style. From pinstripes to plaid, build your wardrobe on little things that express your individuality. Remember, we'll love you even if you show up for a date wearing pleated khakis, no-lace pleather shoes, and an oversized T-shirt. We might not like the clothes, but we'll still love you. We'll just love you even more if you think about what you're wearing before you put it on.

#50: Turn off the Lights when you Leave a Room

#51: Teach a Kid to Ride a Bike

#52 Befriend a chimp while searching for a long-lost sibling on the streets of Mumbai

#53: Choose Between the Woman You Love and Saving Thousands of Innocent Lives

By Patrick Van Slee

You may save hundreds—or even thousands—of lives every week of every month of the year. But you never know when some lunatic is going to come along with a sadistic choice. Right? Make it easy on yourself: Go with the woman you love. Both of you eventually will get over how you allowed thousands of innocents to give up the ghost. Even if you're haunted by their desperate terrified faces night after night, you will always have your woman to tell you there was nothing you could do, that people die every day, that you can't save them all, and you can't hold yourself responsible. Then you can go out for a nice romantic dinner.

Of course, this assumes that there is *no way* you can save both parties. Only you can be the judge of your abilities in this matter. I'm not here to tell you how to do your job, only to save you precious time. The principle benefit of following my advice is that you will not waste valuable milliseconds fretting over what, what, what to do while Lunatic A watches with vicious glee. You'll need these milliseconds to make sure, once again, that there is *no way* you can save both parties.

The same logic that applies to thousands of lives holds true for millions, or even billions, of innocent lives. Once you get to a certain number, it all just starts to feel like statistics, anyway. Which is not to say that the death of so many people should be overlooked, but keep things in perspective. You have a choice to make. Once again, I'm here to save you time, not to play the numbers game. Even if we're talking about the mass extinction of every human being on the planet except for you and your woman...theoretically, you'll still have someone with whom to kick start the human race again. And don't worry, after a few generations, the negative effects of intra-familial coupling become negligible, and you might even create some interesting variations along the way.

Good luck.

#54: LOOK GOOD IN A SPEEDO

By Greg Kemp

Wearing a Speedo might seem like an unmanly thing to do, but there are exceptions. Take an Olympic swimmer, for example. Ask any woman and she'll tell you an Olympic swimmer is a master of the nuthugger. Let's assume you swim more like a tank than Michael Phelps. In that case, successful Speedo-wearing behavior is dictated by geography. If you are within the borders of the United States and its territories, there are only two cases in which you can successfully wear a Speedo.

Case I

Twenty cheerleaders invite you to a private pool party. One of them slips out of her bikini bottoms and wants to see you in it. She calls it a Speedo. You don't argue semantics.

Case II

You are delusional. You think you look best sitting in a beach chair in your Speedo with your hands behind your head and your armpit hair streaming in the wind. In your mind, the chicks aren't looking at those disgusting thick pubes poking out from under the Speedo, but at that bulge they wish they could get their hands on. And when those college-age beach bunnies tip their heads back and roll their eyes, it's not because they think you look like an idiot sitting there with your gut and man-tits, but because they're overwhelmed by orgasms brought on by fantasies of you. For you, Delusional Man, Speedo-wearing success is independent of reality. It's in your head. So party on, brother.

For those of you who want someone other than yourself to think you look good in a Speedo, your best bet is to go to Europe. Fat, hairy, jaundiced—Europe is so diverse that there is a country for every body type. This allows you to blend in with your foreign brethren. Once you blend, you can focus on what's important: Making your package look primo.

Blending In

Before you buy a ticket to Europe, you need to match your body type to a country. This requires self-assessment. Strip down to nothing, and give yourself a good look in the mirror. Does it look like you're hiding behind a grizzly bear? The Southern European countries, such as Italy and Greece, are a lot more forgiving about body hair. Next, look at your gut. Which hangs lower: your stomach or the end of your johnson? The old Eastern Bloc countries have a higher percentage of lard asses, so try Hungary or Bulgaria. The Ukraine is good if you'd also like to visit Chernobyl (real men aren't afraid of nuclear radiation). Now, look at your skin. Are you the color of an albino Chihuahua? Go to the UK, and bring SPF 50.

The Focal Point of the Speedo

You've picked a European country that suits you. You're going to look like every other guy on the beach. Now you need to focus on the presentation of your package. As a general guideline, any area that doesn't bulge is a death blow to a Speedo. If it ruffles in the wind, everyone will think it's because you're not man enough to fill the space. Buying a small Speedo is the obvious answer, but be careful. You don't want to compress whatever goods you're planning to show. And, while women will never admit it, seeing a guy in a Speedo is their one chance to do a full assessment of you. They'll be eyeing your goods every chance they get. They won't be as obvious as you are when you size up their hooters, but they'll be looking. You want a package worthy of having its own beach towel.

Now, if your genes are equine-rich, just fold it over a few times and you're good to go. But statistics show that most men are working with three flaccid inches and a sack the size of a cue ball. That's no formula for looking good. There are two ways to look big down there. You can have a buddy rat-tail one of your testicles with a wet washcloth, and watch it swell up to the size of a soccer ball, or you can get some blood flowing to your member. Getting a sustainable woody on the beach can be tricky business. I don't care who you are, staying big for hours requires meds. Plan ahead and feign erectile dysfunction with a doctor who respects privacy laws. Get a 20-pack of Sildenafil (labeled with brand names such as Viagra and Revatio). Be sure to bring your prescription to Europe; you don't want some impotent border guard confiscating your secret weapon.

Speedo Success

Let's assume you've made it to a European country where you blend in successfully. It's beach day, and you're going to show your stuff. It usually takes up to an hour for Viagra to give you the fullness the chicks seek. And don't be fooled, the erection just doesn't occur. You need to get it started. Before breakfast, pick up a bottle of vodka, swap it for a look at some young Russian's tits, and then head to the beach. Don't be alarmed if takes up to four hours to get happy—that's normal for some people. If you experience sudden vision loss, call a doctor. While these drugs are great at making boners, they are also known to deny blood to the optic nerve and can leave you blind.

Now, the most important lesson: you've taken the pills, and you've seen a good set of melons—so before it gets too big, fold it over like a flip phone, and snap the Speedo closed. As the area fills with blood, everything stays in position, so that your package will look bigger than ever. It might be uncomfortable with the fold in it, but you're a man. You can handle it. But be aware of the dreaded pop-out. If you lose the flip-phone position, the whole system breaks down in seconds. You've got only two choices then: run away and hide, revealing to the world you are a complete coward, or drop trow and strut around the beach looking for someone with whom to joust.

#55: READ

SECTION III:

THE TRICKY MAN

Tips for Getting Away with Almost Anything

#56: GET AWAY WITH ALMOST NEVER GOING TO THE LAUNDROMAT

By Patrick Van Slee

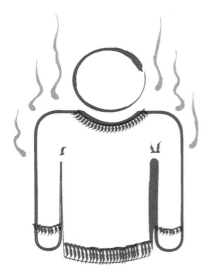

Not everyone can get away with almost never going to the Laundromat. Some people just congenitally stink. Not much they can do about it —they just do. It could be that their diet has way too much beef in it. Who knows?

You know who you are if you smell like garbage all the time, so you might as well just stop reading this article, because it's not going to help you. The rest of you need to admit to yourselves that laundry is an unnecessary waste of time, and then you will be ready to accept the following sage advice.

The first thing you need to realize is that certain types of clothing last longer than others, as far as how long it takes for them to become unwearable. Keeping this in mind, let's start at the outermost layers and work our way in toward the gritty unmentionables.

Sweaters

Sweaters are great, because you almost always wear at least one or two shirts underneath. Consider this Rule One: multiple layers act as a buffer for your stench. Plus, sweaters don't wrinkle. Not everybody is a sweater person, but I highly recommend that you keep a couple of them lying around.

Since the weave of a sweater is much looser than most other clothing, all you have to do if it's carrying that musty, rusty-iron dirty laundry smell is wave it around outside for a second. Take it by the shoulders and give it a good flick to shake the lint and dust free, being careful to avert your head so the dust doesn't get into your eyes and lungs. You might want to let it wave in the breeze for a minute. This allows the sweater to absorb the fresh scent of nature, to replace the foul odor of you.

Button-Downs

You know, dress shirts. Again, these are advantageous because there is another shirt underneath (see Rule One). And they mostly look real sharp—all you have to do is button yourself up, and the whole package is 300 percent neater. It's like making your bed. No matter how much crap you've got lying all over the place in your room, as soon as you make the bed, the place looks as neat as a showroom at IKEA. But the problem with dress shirts is that they wrinkle easily. It's the only item of clothing that can give you away at a glance. There are a couple of ways to get around this mess.

First, if you have to take a shower anyway, you can hang the shirt in the bathroom to steam it out. This also attacks the stink, if there is an odor, which there more than likely is. Steaming your shirt in this way slightly relaxes the fibers, so the sharp creases of the wrinkles won't be as obvious. Plus, because you yourself are freshly clean from your shower, there is the illusion that you have actually just washed the shirt, too. It is possible for you to go through the whole day happily deluded in this way.

Next, there are actual physical ways to cover a large portion of the surface of the shirt. Remember: This is a dress shirt. You can accessorize. That's what they're for. Let's say a few weeks ago you went straight from work to Demon Dogs, that tasty hotdog joint right underneath the train station. You ordered yourself a nice, big, double dog, and drowned it in that yellow crap that someone somewhere decided to call "cheeze," and then you piled on all kinds of onions, peppers, and tomatoes. You grabbed a stool over by the window, so you could watch the people waiting out in the cold for the bus. There you were, munching on your cheezy double dog and fries, absently dipping your hand repeatedly into the paper tray. When you look down to see how many fries are left, you notice that cheeze has drooled all the way down you shirt.

Napkins—even if they are soaked with water—will not remove all evidence of this misadventure when you find it weeks later. This is why God created ties. The wider, the better. Never mind if you think you look like a square. That's right, wrap that thing around your neck, and let it hang down over your cheeze stains, and no one will ever know the difference. In fact, they—whoever they may be—are now quite likely to think you are the kind of guy that goes that extra mile to make an impression. How about that?

Let's not forget suit jackets. Talk about *sharp*. When you're wearing a suit jacket, your dress shirt can be wrinklier than your grandma's grandma, and you'd still cut a fine figure under light scrutiny.

T-Shirts

There are two different kinds of t-shirts: (1) the t-shirt you like, the one that expresses your personality in some way; and (2) the strictly functional t-shirt. The function of a t-shirt is covered by Rule One.

Both types of t-shirts are functional, when you get right down to it, but the key is to have plenty of them. For best results, it is a good idea to get into the habit of wearing two t-shirts at once. This may sound silly and redundant if you aren't used to the idea, but think about it for a second. Double the buffer, first of all (see Rule One again). And second, you already have your wardrobe picked out for the next couple of days. If you are going to be seeing the same people tomorrow, just turn the whole ensemble inside out! Now you still have two t-shirts, and there you are with a whole new outfit. If you don't like wearing t-shirts inside out, then take the extra step and readjust the outer layer, but you should be aware that wearing t-shirts inside out is not forbidden. Who cares? It doesn't look all that different, really. And it will hide other cheeze or guacamole stains, for the most part. Don't cheat yourself by limiting your options.

This brings me to Rule Two: who says you have to change your clothes every day? What's a day but hours stacked onto other hours?

Pants

Depending on your personal preference and monetary situation, you may have any number of different kinds of pants. Some pants don't hold up well after many days of consecutive duty, and some pants can go practically forever without being washed at all. The longer they can go without being washed, the more difficult they are to get clean when they start to rot, if they can get clean at all. Whatever kind of pants you like, don't think that white pants are sharp. They're not. Go with dark tones. Dark tones will hide almost everything, and even if there are visible stains, they usually blend in well and make it look like you live an active lifestyle, which is respectable and interesting.

As I mentioned, some pants hold up better than others. Denim jeans are the most rugged. They were, in fact, originally designed—at least according to my eighth-grade history teacher—by Enrico Levi, who also invented the cotton gin, to stand up to the rigors faced by the wealth-seekers of the Great American Gold Rush of 1492. He made more money than most of the bozos out there ripping up the earth and panning the rivers, because the other fortune hunters had to give all their gold to him when they found their flimsy cotton pants hanging off of their asses in shredded bits and pieces.

Jeans are great for long-term use, but they are difficult to wash. You can't really get around having to throw them in the washing machine, and if you wear them like they were designed to be worn—which is to say, all the time—they need to go in more than once. The next thing you know, you've been sitting in a Laundromat for hours, wondering who the hell thought it was a good idea to seal the television behind a plate of Plexiglas so no one could turn the damn thing off, or at least turn down the volume.

I suggest staying away from jeans altogether. This leaves you cotton, wool, and polyester from which to choose. Corduroy is another option, I suppose, but I don't know anything about corduroy pants, and I'm not even sure how to spell "corduroy," so forget them. Of the three, polyester is the sturdiest; wool, the warmest; and cotton, the most comfortable.

As I said, wool pants are nice and warm when you are outside, but you sweat them up after sitting inside for any length of time, because they are *too* warm. After only two days they start to smell like a dirty sock. They're not very comfortable, anyway. In fact, I don't think very many people even really wear wool pants. Stay away from them, too.

Cotton pants are okay, but they wear out easily, and they are usually expensive. Eventually, that faded spot on your knee or your ass will fray into a little tear, and then the tear will open into a small hole, and then the hole will widen every time you wear them, and then they are no good. Holes in denim jeans are alright, because it looks like you earned them, but holes in cotton pants look dumb.

Which leaves polyester pants. Polyester pants are made from scientific chemicals, and they don't biodegrade. So they're a lot like plastic. Seven million years from now, any galaxy-trotting alien archaeologists digging through the endless mountains of fast-food containers and plastic water bottles are bound to find pockets of polyester pants planted in the ground like rose-bulbs all over the planet. If you don't believe me, slap on some poly pants and drop a cigarette in your lap. The burning ash just pushes the material out of the way, leaving a little cauterized hole that never gets any bigger.

Polyester pants can last at least a lifetime. When you drip cheeze on them, all you have to do is wait for it to dry, and you can scrape it off with your fingernail. But the best thing about polyester pants is that the stink molecules don't like to bond with the artificial fibers. There is no need to put them in a washing machine to get them tolerably scentless. Further explanation about how to treat them once the stink has invaded appears in a later section.

Socks and Shorts

You can usually wear socks for three or four days in a row before the soles start to get stiff with dried sweat, unless you have shoes that don't breathe very well, in which case that could happen after only one day. You can still wear the socks once this happens, but be aware that, because the sweat from your feet no longer has anywhere to go, it feels like you are walking on slime all day long. One way to prolong the life of a single sock is by simply rotating it, so the softer cotton is on the bottom of your foot and the black, stiff, slimy soiled part is on the crest of your foot.

As for the shorts, here are some important things to remember if you want them to last a long time without having to wash them:

- Have lots of them.

- Remember what your mama taught you: be sure to wipe your ass good and clean after heavy business, or any business at all.

- Why wear them to bed? Get soft sheets, if it bothers you.

The Bathroom Sink

Following these important guidelines prevents you from having to bother with laundry for a few months, but eventually your own filthy habits are going to catch up to you. When you find yourself sleeping naked because every single article of clothing you own, with the possible exception of that stupid ankle sock that keeps popping up, is utterly unpleasant to behold—let alone wear—there is no alternative but to do some washing. But fear not! This does not mean you are bound for the Laundromat.

Instead, pick out the clothes you plan to wear tomorrow, and haul them up to your bathroom sink. An extra pair of socks wouldn't hurt, while you're at it. Turn on the water, adjusting it to a comfortable temperature. Do *not* plug it up. The water is just going to get filthy, and you will be working against yourself if you let the clothes sit in a pool of dirty water.

Stuff the pants into the sink. Soap is not necessary. After they have absorbed as much water as they will hold, grasp the pants with both hands, with your fingers fanned out as wide as possible. Then squeeze your hands closed as if to make a fist. Watch with satisfaction as the water turns black. Release the pants, allow the fabric to soak up more water briefly, grasp them in another spot and squeeze again, this time slightly raising them from the surface of the bowl as you find a new grip. This practice allows the filthy water that has begun to collect to drain away. As you continue to knead the pants, pockets of air form, with little bubbles gurgling out of the fabric. This is good—the bubbles help to loosen the dirt, and it makes a cool gurgling noise.

Soon the water begins to turn from black to brown or gray. When this happens, just toss the pants into the bathtub, and repeat this process with your shirts and shorts. There is no way that you are going to get all of the filth out from your pants, so just be happy with them not smelling horrible anymore.

Your socks require a bit more attention. They are going to stink much, much worse than anything you would ever want to go near. Turn on the hot water, and just throw them in the bowl. Don't even touch them; leave them alone for a few minutes. When the air in the bathroom starts to fill with a hint of stink, deal with it. When the socks plug up the drain, let them. After the bowl is just about filled, turn off the water. Wait a few minutes, then add some cold water into the steaming soup of socks, plunge your hands inside, pull the socks away from the drain, and let the water seep away. Turn the water back on, adjusting the temperature so it is comfortable again.

This is the only part where you might benefit from a little bit of soap, although it is definitely not necessary. If the soles of your socks are black, there's simply no way to make them look nice and new again; it's way too late for that. But if for some reason you are struck with an inexplicable desire to attack the stain, knock yourself out. Plant the sock lengthways along the surface of your palm, and rub the soap on the black stain until you feel little or no friction. When you are through messing around with the soap, hold the socks one at a time under the water and begin to knead them as you did your other clothing. There is no need to wait for them to reabsorb water between successive squeezes; the socks are small and porous enough to become re-saturated almost immediately following each squeeze. Continue to do this until the soap is used up and bubbles that fall into the sink pop right away.

I know it's probably getting late by this point, because you have undoubtedly waited until 20 minutes past the time you told yourself you needed to go to sleep before admitting that this washing procedure had to be done. One last thing, and then you are ready to go to sleep: You need to know how to wring out your sort-of clean clothes.

Wring the Sock

You have to wring out your clothes as thoroughly as possible, because you are going to let them hang dry in the bathroom, and you have only six or seven hours until you need to wear them. Each article of clothing can be wrung in a similar way, so I'm going to use the socks to illustrate. This is a very meditative motion. It can help you in all kinds of ways you can't even imagine right now. Trust me.

1. Fold the wet sock in half.

2. Grasp one end with your right fist in front of your face, palm away from you, leaving no part of the sock peaking above your pinky finger.

3. Hooking your left fist toward you, grasp the sock just below your right fist.

4. Push the sock away from you, gradually unfurling both your arms and bending your wrists toward their opposite orientation. As you do this, water streams out. Be sure to leave the right wrist above the left, so that the wrung part of the sock remains above the as yet un-wrung part, and gravity does not re-soak your work.

The Dryer

There is a pretty good chance that you waited to do all of this washing until just before you had to leave for the day. If this is the case, you are doomed to walk around wearing chilly, wet (but astoundingly fresh!) clothes for the next couple of hours, until your body heat dries the moisture. Don't worry about what people might think; you can just tell them you fell in a lake or something.

Unfortunately, your shoes aren't going to let your feet off so easily. Wet socks tend to stay wet when the moisture has no place to go. You could walk around with soggy feet all day, or you could nuke your socks real quick before you run out, taking a moment to thank the universe for the convenience of modern kitchen appliances.

After you've adequately wrung your socks, either place them on a relatively clean ceramic dinner plate or make sure that the floor of the microwave is clear of pizza grease, and set the timer for about one-and-a-half minutes. Open the microwave door to release the steam and repeat the process until the socks are dry to taste.

May your pile of laundry continue to bear ripe fruit. It's too bad we aren't covered with fur like apes or cheetahs. Then none of this hassle would be necessary.

#57: Fake your Own Death

#58: Date Two Girls at the Same Time

By Ryan Placchetti

Dispelling the Sitcom Myth

If you've turned on a television set in the last 30 years, you've probably seen that sitcom staple: a guy gets in over his head trying to date two women at once. The scenario is almost always the same, whether the character is an overwhelmed nerd or a well-oiled philandering machine. By the end of the episode, there's a man stuck in a restaurant with two beautiful women and one humiliating life lesson. The hero is exposed as a fraud—humiliated and ultimately rejected by both ladies. His hubris is laid bare for the sake of a cautionary tale about the dangers of an overextended libido. Television networks would like us to think that honesty is the best policy, which is dubious advice at best, and in this instance, totally contrary the male prerogative: getting laid.

Sitcom life is crowded, because events take place over the finite span of a half-hour. In reality, your window of opportunity is a bit more accommodating. Let's assume you're a very busy man, working 60 hours a week. Let's also assume you get the recommended eight hours of sleep a night. That translates to 12 hours of work and eight hours of sleep every weekday, with the weekend off. During the week, you have four hours of free time a day, and on the weekends, you have 16 hours a day. That gives you 20 hours of weekday time, and 32 hours of weekend time. Trying to schedule two women into 52 hours of free time is like trying to sink a three-point shot into an Olympic-sized swimming pool. In other words, it's not that hard, especially if you create a schedule for each woman. Regardless of what your actual schedule is, make sure that you're never available to both women at the same time. Assign each woman an iron-clad block of time, and only adjust it in the event of a booty-call emergency.

There is *no excuse* for both women ending up in the same restaurant at the same time on the same day. Myth dispelled.

Location, Location

So how can you avoid getting caught? Choose your targets carefully. I sympathize with the strong compulsion to pour your syrupy charm on every short stack of hotness in sight, but you've got to learn how to think strategically. Make sure there's no way for both ladies to meet each other, either professionally or socially. Both women should be geographically separated—from you and from each other. They should be far enough apart to shop at different places and go to different bars. Just because women aren't rational doesn't mean that they're stupid. They have keen senses when it comes to figuring out which floozy is trying to shimmy up to their man.

Never take either girl home, if you can help it. You've gone to great lengths to keep the girls apart—why give them common ground? Go back to her place, and do it on a pile of stuffed animals instead. Besides, if one of them finds out you've been doing her wrong, it would probably be best if she didn't know exactly where you live. Acrylic nails hurt.

Naming Conventions

Give your ladies androgynous or even masculine nicknames. Chrissy becomes Chris, Lucy becomes Lou, Kiki become Jeff. Do this until you're used to saying their dude-onyms, and they're used to responding in kind. If you get a call from Kiki during a date with Melody, and you call her Jeff, you might save face with Mel, but Kiki is going to smell blood—unless you've already prepared the ground. By establishing your strangely evasive routines early, no one will ever call you on it later in the game.

If You Still Don't Get It...

If—despite all this wisdom—you'd like to try meeting both girls at the same restaurant, at the same time, memorize these tips now:

The first thing every man needs is another dude in his corner: a wingman. Get in good with a waiter or a bartender; he can help you out in a pinch. Wear clothes you don't mind trashing, since there's a good chance of getting food, drink, or blood on them. And order small portions; you're going to be eating two dinners.

When you need to get away from the table, the obvious excuse is the bathroom—but unless you want to fake a urinary tract infection, this deception won't hold up long. You can get away with a bathroom trip only every 20 minutes or so. Don't worry—be clever.

Remember that server with whom you made friends? Ask him to spill something on you—preferably water—and squeeze in an extra bathroom trip to dry off or clean up. You can use this technique to get away from one table, and use the stain as an excuse for an extended absence from the other table. You can double the mileage out of a stain just by keeping your wits sharp. A nasty marinara splash can buy you up to 15 minutes away from each table. Don't forget, you're not the only one at the table wearing clothes. If you need some time, or she's just getting a little too suspicious of your itty-bitty bladder, signal your wingman on the inside and have him drop a mustard bomb on her blouse. That's another 20 minutes.

Don't forget: If the manager hasn't caught on to your double-dipping antics, you can probably get one of your dates paid for by the restaurant, if you make enough of a fuss. Trying to get both dates on the house is a quick way to get ratted out by middle-management. Don't even try it, unless you brought your fake mustache.

Finally, get out quickly. Fake an emergency if you have to, and go home alone. Do not leave with either girl. Arrange to meet your favorite somewhere else later, or arrange to meet both at staggered times throughout the night. It's all up to you at this point, smooth operator.

So what do you do if you drop the ball? One word: containment. There are a few ways to go here. Option one: propose a threesome. You're already in hot water, why not? Their answer might surprise you, but probably not. Either way, your brazen lack of respect for women should paralyze them long enough for you to bolt. Option two: just run. Don't look back; just run. Let them worry about the check, and let your wingman delay them. Option three: pick a girl. Tell her she's the one you really liked all along, and explain how agreeing to go on a date with the other girl was really just a cunning ploy to introduce her to your friend…the waiter. Obviously, the third option is your best bet, and it rewards the manly solidarity of your wingman.

A Word of Caution

With great risk comes great reward. But when you date two women at the same time, you're gambling with your love life and your reputation. If you get caught, both women will know what a scumbag you are, and they're not going to shut up about it. Short of wining and dining conjoined twins, the odds of you getting away with dating two women at a time are pretty slim.

#59: Execute a Bribe

By William Tiernan

There's nothing more satisfying than making the impossible possible. Car about to get towed? Don't think so. No more tickets to the concert of the year? Not if you can help it. Accidentally backed over your neighbors' mailbox in front of their eight-year-old kid? They'll never know it was you. How do you pull off these seemingly miraculous feats? Easy, my friend: Find the squeaky wheel, and apply some grease. The most effective grease on the market? Cold, hard cash.

Before discussing the details of the bribe—who to bribe, when, and how—let's settle on an appropriate amount. Here are the choices:

1. **The single.** Two can get you a few Sausage McMuffins on a hung-over Saturday morning, and a George Washington is the staple currency at strip clubs. As a bribing currency however, the dollar is impotent. Ever try sliding a few bills to a meter maid to get out of a parking ticket? That can't even buy her four donuts.

2. **The five spot.** The five-dollar bill exists solely for tipping—from the valet at P.F. Chang's (where your girlfriend made you go for your six-month anniversary); the cabbie who drove your wasted ass home from the bar; or the barber who cleaned you up with the number-four clippers. But try using a five to get the store manager to overlook the six-pack of Budweiser he caught you shoplifting because you gambled away your paycheck playing

Internet roulette, and you'll be exposed for what you are—a cheap bastard. A $5 bribe is an equivocal gesture, one that will be snuffed out, not taken seriously, and easily shrugged off with a disapproving stare. It's what you might call an "Are you serious?" bribe.

3. **The ten.** It's got some influencing power, but it has two weaknesses. First, those new ten-dollar bills are purple, and resemble Monopoly money. Subtly pass one to the lady whose Prius you just rear-ended in the parking lot of the Dollar Store, and she'll probably mistake it for a chic business card. Second, the ten is a "favor" bill. Favors are different than bribes. You hand a ten to the photo technician at Walgreens if you want your pictures developed in 10 minutes; you don't hand one to the judge presiding over your DWI case.

4. **The twenty.** Andrew Jackson is on the twenty, and he was a bad-ass, Indian-fighting machine who kept company with Davy Crockett. A twenty can get you and your buddies past a pro-female bouncer, or even into a minor sporting event without a ticket. Two or three years ago, I would have argued that the twenty was *the* perfect bribing bill. But in today's wretched economy, the twenty doesn't carry the same weight it did in 2005. Try dropping a twenty on a rich bastard flying in first class to get his seat, and his first thought will be: This won't even cover 1/100th of my monthly gas bill for my Magnum speedboat. And with the dollar in the gutter of the global economy, you need something more potent than a twenty to buy off the Indonesian cop who wants to throw you in the slammer for pitching your gum on the sidewalk.

5. **The fifty.** The fifty is the ultimate bribing bill. Consider first the fifty-dollar bill's president, Ulysses S. Grant. Grant coined the term "lobbyist"—using it to describe the political movers and shakers who hung out in the lobby of the Willard Hotel in Washington DC,

seeking presidential favors. And what's a lobbyist but a glorified briber? The fifty is all about business—albeit behind-the-scenes, smoky-back-room business. It's the John Rocker of bribes: shady and unsophisticated, but one hell of a closer. And it lends itself well to the principle of supply and demand; like a good Keanu Reeves movie—which you don't see one very often—its rarity sweetens its appeal.

6. **The hundred.** If you're wondering about the one hundred-dollar bill, let me say this. A c-note is a heavy hitter, but it's not suited for bribing. For starters, Benjamin Franklin is on the one hundred, and he was a diplomat, statesman, and a stand-up guy in general. Second, the hundred is ostentatious; it's a "gift" bill—something you might give to the doctor who delivers your baby, or to your son for graduating from college. But a $100 bribe could be viewed as "pretentious" and might backfire, as in: "I don't need your hundred bucks, you rich bastard"—even if you're not rich and your intentions are legit. Think of the difference between the hundred and the fifty this way: in Las Vegas, professional athletes at the Palms throw around one hundred-dollar bills; professional poker players at Binions play with fifties.

Preparation

The $50 bribe is a "once every six months" transaction. If you don't have a generous grandma who is fond of sending you a $50 bill for every major holiday, go to the bank and get fifty bucks. I'm not talking about two twenties, a ten, a five, four ones and a bunch of loose change. Ask the teller for a crisp, shiny fifty. Tuck it away in your wallet—out of sight but easily accessible.

Target

Last June, I stashed a Grant in my wallet in preparation for an opportunity to bribe someone. Soon after, I got pulled over for speeding. Unfortunately, you can't drop a fifty on state employees—or federal employees, for that matter—unless you want to spend some time in jail.

You also don't want to jeopardize your local reputation—if you have one—with a hasty fifty. Suppose your son is about to fail fifth-grade language arts because you didn't help him with his book report about *Where the Red Fern Grows*. You can't bail him out by discretely slipping Mr. Johnson a fifty at Back-to-School night. This is a sure way to get your picture posted on the community watch list and ensure your child a miserable education experience through high school.

So, who can you bribe?

In August, I got my answer. I was sitting around the house, it was 99 degrees, and my air conditioner crapped out. I called an AC company that contracts out repair work. I was pissed, because I knew it was going to cost at least a hundred bucks for the guy to do 10 minutes of repair work that I was too inept to do. Sure enough, Dustin—after eight minutes of work—slid me a bill for $136.25. Dejected, I opened my wallet to grab a spare check and there it was: The fifty, peeking its head out from behind my driver's license, wagging its tail, waiting for a chance to stretch its legs.

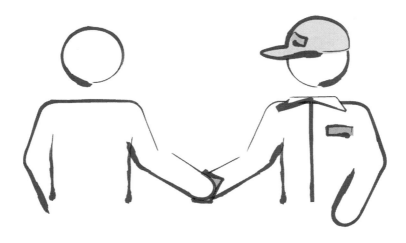

Execution

I hesitated for a minute to assess the situation. Had Dustin entered any information into a computer? If so, he wasn't taking my money, because the computer would tell his boss about the $136.25 job he just finished. Were there any neighbors snooping around? The $50 bribe should be witnessed only by the briber and the bribee. Fortunately, the coast was clear on both fronts.

"So, how much would it take to pretend you were never here?" I asked calmly. Dustin smiled and nodded; I was speaking his language. "You tell me," he said. I paused for a moment; then slowly unsheathed the fifty and presented it to him. He nodded approvingly, gently took it from me, and slid it into his back pocket. Then he handed me a copy of the receipt—the only copy. "Let me know if you have any more problems," he said. With Grant in mind, I stepped inside to get Dustin a Coors Light for the road. Unfortunately, I was out of cigars.

Summary

The opportunity to pull off the $50 bribe is rare. It sneaks up on you—just like age 50—so you've got to be ready. You can't necessarily prepare, but you can be aware of potential opportunities. Here's a cheat sheet for doing it right:

1. Target people who work for—but off-site from—"the man." They're paying for their own gas, they're not making what they deserve, and they're out of the watchful eye of the boss. It's all benefit with almost no risk for them, and you might establish a long-term working relationship.

2. No cameras, computers, or spectators within 500 yards.

3. Don't share your bribing success story with your wife or girlfriend; in the same way she'll never share in your joy over wet T-shirt contests, she won't find the bribe nearly as cool as you did.

4. Crisp bill, folded once.

5. Be discreet; the physical gesture carries as much weight as the verbal offer.

6. Remember, the $50 bill is the king of bribes in this economy because of gas prices. The twenty might get the bribee a half a tank, but with fifty he can fill it up—and still have some money to pick up a pizza for dinner.

7. The $50 bribe is primarily about saving money. It should be used in situations that would regularly put you out between $75 and $200: The towed car, the egregious parking ticket, the broken toilet. It should only be used for access to secure an otherwise $75 or more "ticket" to a prime venue such as Augusta National, a Phish concert, or an upscale Thai massage parlor. It should not be used to get a table at Outback Steakhouse on Friday night. Doing so would make your dinner for two cost $90 instead of $40; you might as well go to Chili's.

8. Most importantly, the $50 bribe is about having fun. They say those big horse races are the best two minutes in sports, but my give and take with Dustin was much better than this year's Belmont. It offered the immediate rush of gambling—but with a much higher success rate. And it provided some good male bonding—a solid business transaction between two guys trying to make and save a few bucks, sealed by a lobbyist-friendly president who's been dead for almost 123 years.

Good Targets for a $50 Bribe

Contract repair men

Meter maids

Airline check-in attendants

Towed-car lot operators

Sporting event and concert ushers

Greedy bosses

Children (for whom a twenty will work fine)

Bad Targets for a $50 Bribe

Teachers

Girlfriends and wives

Judges

Bank tellers

Cops

FBI agents

Casino dealers

Theater ushers

Dear Mr. Man:

My wife wants me to throw away everything I like. Yes, my favorite ball cap is old and faded, but I got it at a Dodgers spring training game back in '88—the year Kirk Gibson smacked Dennis Eckersley's backdoor slider over the right-field wall and the Dodgers won the World Series. The orange recliner she disdains was the first piece of furniture I ever bought; an old geezer at a yard sale thought he was playing hardball with me, but I got it for $50, and he threw in a weed eater. What I'm saying is, I like my stuff— but my wife calls it crap and wants to throw it all away. Doesn't she realize that this stuff means something to me? I'm starting to think she doesn't have a soul.

Signed,
Married to Satan

Dear Married to Satan:

Those are really touching stories. I've got an AC/DC concert shirt from their '86 Fly on the Wall tour. It's awesome. But in just the way men are incapable of understanding why women want flowers unexpectedly—and handwritten notes just because—no woman can understand the value men place on our stuff. There's nothing like our first Member's Only jacket, or the jeans we were wearing when we first got head. I mean, these things are part of us. The stains and the smells are not flaws, but a sign of character. Would you throw away your dog for being stinky and old?

That said, an old pair of socks is not Rex. I'm willing to bet that half the stuff you're keeping really is crap. Think of your girl's needs. She wants to impress her friends when they come over. She wants to be proud of you when you're out. So here's what you gotta do: pick one thing. Choose the recliner, those old sweatpants, or the Key West shot glass, and throw everything else away. When she comes home, announce that you did it for her. Sit her down, and tell her the story of the one thing you decided to keep. If she doesn't well up and cry, or tear off your clothes and rip you to sexual shreds, she really is Satan. You'd better ditch her—quick—and hope the trash truck hasn't taken away all your cool stuff.

Let me know how it goes!

Signed,
Mr. Man

Dear Mr. Man,

I did exactly what you said. Problem is, the one thing I decided to keep was my Hitachi VCR, so I could play homemade porn of old girlfriends. My wife went into a rage, chucked the Hitachi in the pool, and tore my tape collection to pieces. I think she left me. What should I do?

Signed,
Married to Satan

Dear Married to Satan,

Don't worry, it's not as bad as you think. There are specialty electronic stores that can fix your tapes, and they still make VCRs.

Signed,
Mr. Man

#61: Outsmart the Secret Police of a Former Eastern Bloc Nation

#62: GET OUT OF A SPEEDING TICKET

By Bobby Nelson

The police are an essential part of any functional community. Most cops show the bravery, valor, and hardiness that keep us safe from the dregs of society—drug dealers, rapists, murderers, and other nefarious characters. However, as the early-90s rap group NWA can tell you, the cops aren't always your buddies. Evidence? The speeding ticket.

Let me play driver's education teacher for a moment. The best way to get out of a ticket is to avoid it before it happens. Drive defensively, and don't speed. Simple, right? Well, the best way to avoid a venereal disease is to abstain from casual sex, and we all know how simple that is. Telling a man to stop speeding is pointless. You'd have better luck ordering a dolphin to stop getting wet.

You're going to speed, and eventually you're going to get caught. When this happens, you have a choice. You can cooperate fully, take the ticket, and in the process, set the world record for chirping "Yes, sir!" the most in a given period of time. Or you can prevent your next paycheck from going to the kibble fund of the local K-9 unit by utilizing "The Method," an ingenious technique I have crafted and put into use during no fewer than seven routine traffic stops. How well does The Method work? It has gotten me off the hook six times, and failed me only once, when the cop stuck me with a financial burden that hampered happy hour for weeks.

To successfully execute The Method, you must learn to fake agonizing groin pain. If you don't trust your acting ability, a solid punch to your grapes will do the trick. Your facial expression is the key to success. Tuck your lips behind your teeth and wince. When the officer asks, "Do you know why I pulled you over?" nod your head. Look away, as if the pain from your groin is soothed only by the sight of the four pennies stuck to the bottom of your cup holder. When he asks if you're okay, answer in a solemn tone: "Look, officer, I know this sounds incredibly weird, but I've really got to get somewhere so I can pass this kidney stone."

The kidney stone is the marshmallow in The Method's s'mores— without it, the whole thing falls apart. To make The Method airtight, you must understand the kidney stone inside and out. Kidney stones, or *renal calculi,* are hard aggregations left behind by minerals in urine. These small stones—usually five millimeters in diameter—take the usual urinary path through the urethra, before being expelled with excruciating pain through the tip of the penis. If you suffer from kidney stones, expect to give birth to a rock nearly the size of a bullet. By the time it's through with you, you'll wish you could put the thing in a gun, and end your suffering.

Most men cringe at the thought of these urethral urchins; cops are no exception. Hence, the success of The Method. The first time I used The Method, it worked so well, the officer actually stepped into the road to make sure I could get into traffic safely and on my way home to "pass my stone." Another time, the cop in question had passed his own kidney stones just two months before.

The Method, however, isn't completely fool-proof. It may even become such a big deal to the cop that he calls in a MediVac helicopter to airlift you to the nearest hospital. It turns out that a helicopter ride and doctor's bill are just a tad more expensive than a speeding ticket. Even if you don't get sent to the ER, you could be looking at increased fines, or even jail time for lying to a cop. Despite these negative consequences, The Method has produced positive concrete results, so it is worth a try if you want to keep some of your hard-earned dead presidents.

Let's just hope no cops read this. Happy speeding, gents.

#63: Avoid Chores in High-Traffic Areas

By Nancy R. Hatch

Disclaimer: If you find genuine satisfaction in using your brain and your brawn to complete chores around the house, and achieve an inner glow when your significant other smiles in appreciation, then the following ideas are not necessarily for you. But if you revel in the feeling of "getting away with something"—at least some of the time—read on.

Note: For these tips to work properly, you need to find a mate who puts up with your amusing antics, such as pretending not to remember where the forks are kept.

As a general rule, inside chores located in high-traffic areas are not for you. Let the rest of the family divvy them up. Instead, focus your time and talents in areas of the house where no one can see what you are doing. When you devote your efforts to cleaning less visible areas of the house (like the attic, basement, and garage), you will be able to spend more time doing what you want to do, and less time working.

Vacuuming the House

Let's face it: unless you're certifiably OCD, vacuuming is a thankless chore. No one notices the absence of grit on carpeted surfaces. They only notice when the grit reappears. So, avoid volunteering to vacuum anything in high-traffic areas. You should, however, get involved in the vacuum-purchase decision. Buy the noisiest machine on the market. Wait until your wife is engaged in some quiet activity that requires concentration. Rev up your bad boy, and start taking it for a spin around the living room. As soon as your wife yells, "Honey, don't do that right now! I'll do it tomorrow," turn the machine off, give it a pat on the head, and send it back to bed. Now, go ahead and engage in some quiet activity all your own.

Dusting

Avoid this chore with every fiber of your being. No one looks around a freshly dusted room and says, "Wow! All the dust is gone. Steve sure did a good job." No, sir. This is not the chore for you. To avoid getting drafted for dusting detail, make sure that the first time you dust is the last time you are asked to dust. Just put everything that you moved while dusting back in exactly the wrong spot. Put smaller items, like picture frames, behind larger items, like lamps—and make sure the bowl that holds the house keys winds up as far away from the front door as possible.

Doing the Laundry

If the washer and dryer are located in a remote area of the house, or are located off-site, you should consider volunteering for this task. Machines do virtually all the work for you, freeing you to play videogames, read a book, smoke a cigar, or lift weights. The downside of this chore is that the result of shoddy work is readily apparent. If your son's briefs turn pink because you washed them with a red polo shirt, he is not going to suffer in silence. If you decide to volunteer for this task, your significant other immediately jumps at the chance to walk you through the basics of sorting and folding, so we won't waste your time here. Note: if the laundry facilities are in the middle of the kitchen, or another high-traffic area of the home, make sure to turn your son's briefs pink—or shrink your wife's favorite shirt—the first time you do the laundry. You won't be asked again.

Taking Out the Garbage

When you see that the garbage is getting full, take it out. Every time. Why? This is a high-traffic chore that pays real rewards and has virtually no downside. You pick up a bag that weighs a pound or two, walk it to the appropriate receptacle, and toss it in. It takes seconds, and you cannot do it wrong. No one is going to walk behind you to make sure you throw the garbage away correctly. You are never going to hear, "Honey, when I throw away the garbage, I really like the coffee grounds and banana peels to stay on top, with paper goods on the bottom." This chore is your chance to shine with incredibly low effort.

Cooking Dinner

When your spouse has a tough day, offer to make dinner. But, remember the kitchen is a high-traffic area. Don't get too familiar with it. As a general rule, stay out of the kitchen entirely, except to fuel your body or quench your thirst. As you start to prepare dinner, think ahead about what you are going to need, and ask your wife where she keeps those items. Don't worry if whether you already know where a specific item is. Ask anyway. "Honey, I can't find the colander?" "Sweetheart, do we have chili powder?" "Darling, where do you keep the pots and pans?" When she's had enough of your ridiculous questions, she's guaranteed to shoo you out of the kitchen and finish dinner herself.

Emptying the Dishwasher

Emptying the dishwasher is no fun. The dishes are already clean, so there's no satisfying feeling of a job well-done; and as long as the door to the dishwasher is closed, no one can even tell whether it's empty or full. Here's how to get out of it: put a few essential items away in the wrong place, where your loved one is sure to see them. "Why would he put the mixing bowls in the pantry? That makes no sense." As soon as you are done emptying the dishwasher, return to your domain, where no one will be able to see you taking a nap.

Cleaning the Basement or the Attic

Now, this is the chore for you! Far from the general flow of traffic, you can enjoy yourself while you straighten things up. Wait for a miserable day when the weather outside is not fit for man or beast. Set up a work station—including a chair, a table, a small TV, and a cooler of beer. Take a break, and watch some TV. If you hear any footsteps approaching, stand up and shuffle some clutter around. Leave the TV on. It's there to keep you company. Straighten that pile of boxes that was taunting you out of the corner of your eye. Once your spouse and kids have left the area, take another break. After several hours, get up, turn off the TV, and head to the main level, "Hon, I'm going to take a break. I've made some headway, but not as much as I'd hoped. I'll try and finish it up next week." Note: if you do not have a garage, attic, or basement, find some other area to call your own, a den, office, study, or walk-in closet is perfect. Just make sure that it's out of the general runway pattern of the home.

Pool Maintenance

If you have a pool, people expect it to be clean all the time. Like making a bed, it has to be done every day, even if it's going to get dirty again. In that way, it differs from the attic, garage, or office, where the general expectation is to see some degree of clutter. If possible, refuse to put in a pool until the kids are old enough to swim (and take care of it themselves). But what if you've found a perfect house, with a pool smack-dab in the middle of the backyard? Go ahead and buy it. You're a man. That pool is no match for you. As soon as you move in, head to the pool store. Get the best self-cleaning vacuum that you can afford. You deserve it. Get a few key instructions, and take that bad boy home. For the rest of the summer, let the vacuum roam gently along the subtle contours of your pool, massaging away dirt, while you apply similar moves to your wife in the bedroom. Finally, you've found a type of activity around the house for which you're uniquely qualified.

#64: FART LOUDLY IN THE PRESENCE OF ROYALTY AND ACT LIKE IT WASN'T YOU

#65: TAKE A SHORT CUT

#66: LISTEN WITHOUT LISTENING

By Eric Camarillo

I grew up in a house full of women.

As a result, I have internalized many small rules that other men don't get. Here's an example: putting the toilet seat down. To an average guy, this seems like a relatively unimportant thing. Why go through the hassle over and over again, when we can just leave it up? Surely, if the next person to go into the bathroom is a woman, she'll see that the toilet seat is up and put it down herself. Not so. I have seen far too many reasonably intelligent women fall into toilets, and a surprising number of men disappear mysteriously by the end of the week.

The most important thing I learned from having lived with women, however, is how to listen without listening. This technique saves you from many unnecessary discussions—such as your girlfriend's recitation of each notch on her sexual bedpost, the latest round of gossip from her office involving people you know nothing about, or her elaborate plans to remodel the guest bathroom. Follow my simple tips, and you'll soon be able to tune all this out, with none the wiser.

1. When she asks you a question, always pretend to know less than you actually do. You know nothing. Whether she asks about As the World Turns, interior design, or how fashion reflects upon the human condition, act as if you have no idea what she's talking

about—unless you're a real man, in which case you don't have to pretend at all.

2. When a question or topic of discussion comes up, ask her how she feels about the subject. If I've learned anything from living with women, it's this: They love to talk. For example, suppose two men are discussing a burnt light bulb:

"Hey, that light bulb is burnt out."

"Yeah. We should change it."

End of discussion.

Now two women discuss the exact same thing:

"What's wrong with this lightbulb?"

"What do you mean?"

"The light. It won't turn on."

"Are you flicking the switch?"

"Of course I am."

"It might be burnt out."

"Crap. I don't feel like changing it."

"Are you OK?"

"I've just been so tired lately."

"Have you been sleeping?"

"Yeah, but Danny's been such an ass."

"Tell me about it. You wouldn't believe how many times I've asked Joe to put that damn toilet seat down ..."

End of discussion—not because it's actually over, but because it would go on for a few paragraphs, and I'm sure you see my point by now.

3. Always listen for a minute or two before glazing over. You have to gauge her rhythm to punctuate the conversation with the proper frequency and pitch of affirmative noises. Listening to all that gab can be a little fatiguing, the same way your vision starts to blur when you are still playing Warfish at three o'clock in the morning. There is no way to prevent this natural glaze from setting in, but you can keep her from noticing, which is crucial. If she thinks that you're not interested in what she's saying, she'll get all huffy and puffy on you. This can be problematic when dealing with your wife or girlfriend—or your mom, if you're under eighteen or still live at home. After you've established a minute of good listening, go ahead and zone out little by little. But don't forget to pepper the conversation with plenty of phrases such as, "You don't say?" "Wow, really?" "And then?" "No way!" "I don't believe it!" These simple interjections cement her belief that you are, indeed, listening.

4. Make sure to maintain good eye contact. Don't stare her straight in the face, as if you're daring her to tap dance in her underwear—but don't look away too often, and don't stare at a single spot for too long. Try to nod after she makes a point.

Don't be deterred from non-listening if the women in your life catch on after your first few attempts. You'll get better as you practice, and it becomes amazingly simple with time. You'll learn to recognize the changes in her pitch that indicate when she's asking a question, when she's making a point, or when she's making a joke; you'll be able to read her face accurately enough to know when she's being sarcastic, when she's being serious, and when she's just kidding. Combine that knowledge with the skills here, and you may even be able to achieve the coveted title of "good listener."

Disclaimer: As a woman spends more time with you, she will begin to pick up on *your* verbal and physical cues, the same way you will learn hers. Only non-listen when talking about something trivial, and don't non-listen too often. Also, unless you're extremely clever (i.e., smarter than your mom), don't use this technique with the woman who either gave birth to you, raised you, or both.

Another important note: This technique was developed for the sole purpose of helping men avoid needless conversation when speaking with members of the opposite gender. While non-listening can be adapted for use by women when talking to women, any other use of non-listening is prohibited, except where protected by law.

#67: NEGOTIATE

#68: PREVARICATE

#69: RIP ASS IN PUBLIC WITHOUT GETTING ARRESTED

By Patrick Van Slee

Dude, these are dangerous freakin' times. Scary dangerous. Gut-stomping fascists roam the streets, enforcing some new crap-ass law that pops up every other day; people rat each other out for pats on the head; and the Great Eye is always watching, so you can't do nothing without getting in trouble. You can't even rip ass in public anymore without getting arrested.

Until now.

Listen. I got the scoop. You want to know how to rip ass in public without getting arrested? Follow my tried-and-true advice, and you, too, can steal a tiny bit of your freedom back from The Man.

Before we go any further, though, let's get one thing straight: there is only one really good way to rip ass. You need a full-blown, 25-alarm explosion. Bam! Force it out like Steamboat Willie! Chuck it like Charles in Charge! Criminalizing this activity is nothing less than an assault against Mother Nature in all her magnificence.

This being a universal zero-tolerance dystopia, you can forget about packing your *cabeza* with excuses. None of them are going to do you any good when the Ministry of Love gets wind of your deed and breaks out the batons. But if you keep these key factors in mind, you can keep your can out of the clink.

If a Tree Falls in the Forest...

Obviously, if no one hears you rip ass, you didn't. Sure, it would be nice if you could freely rip ass when nobody else was around. But these days, nobody's ever really alone, are they? No. There's always somebody—or something—watching and listening. You may recall the old nursery rhyme:

No more tears

From parents nor peers

The walls are mirrors

Eyes and ears

They'll see and hear

So far and near,

For years and years

And years and years...

So here's what I do: If I'm walking down the street and I get the notion I'm about to blow my cork, I wait a few seconds until the next Acquisitions truck rushes down the street for a fresh load of Freethinkers. Just as it zooms by me, right when the sirens are at their loudest: Ba-DAM! Unless someone is staring right at my ass, watching for my speed suit to puff out like a quadruple amputee trying to escape from a steam tent, I'm all good.

Evasive Maneuvers

The above method won't work if you happen to be out on a Sunday. Oh, yes, you can rip ass on Quietude Day: The day of the week when the fascists are listening their hardest for the sounds we train ourselves all week long to hide—smooch sounds, laughing, cursing. Ripping ass. I'm telling you straight, dude. I do it all the time.

Remember: If you are nowhere near the epicenter of the ass-ripping by the time anyone's senses zero in, you have successfully ripped ass in public. In other words, rip ass on the move.

Letting one fly while suddenly changing direction is a one way to pull this off. As you approach a tight corner, make sure no one is following directly behind you. Wait until the exact moment when you reach the point when the avenues converge—then unleash, turn 90 degrees, and keep walking. Watch with silent glee as your fellow pedestrians are too traumatized to figure out exactly where the offending ba-doom came.

Other great opportunities to rip ass on the move:

- When you are sliding down a brunch, lunch, or "dunch" pole.

- When you are jumping into a chemical inoculation bath.

- When you are being beaten anyway, in which case you'll want to try to time ass ripping to coincide with the officer's grunts.

Hiding in Plain Sight

Ripping ass on the move works well enough, but we spend most of our days indoors. Between Info-Condensing, Historical Erasure, and Ideological Indoctrination classes, you probably find yourself sitting around in public places a lot, surrounded by people who would sic the Torture Brigade on their own mamas for ripping ass.

What to do?

The sounds of blowing out your sinuses and ripping ass are very similar in depth, pitch, and volume. Carry a hanky around with you, and time your ass-ripping so that it coincides with honking out your nose. Be sure not to pull this maneuver if you are sitting very close to a colleague, because the vibration in the seat will give you away.

Accuse the Accuser

Any one of these strategies involves a certain amount of risk. But stay calm, Chilly Willy—if a fellow citizen suspects you of ripping ass, follow this script and watch them clam up:

Them: "Did you just rip ass?"

You: "No way, dude. That was *you.*"

It's our word against theirs, right?

Congratulations. You've just enriched your life by eking out the tiniest sliver of daily freedom. May there come a day when those Party creeps get recalled back to whatever-the-hell dimension from which they were spawned. Until then, let her rip, soldier.

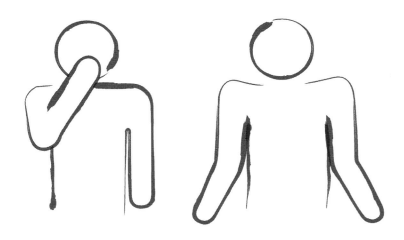

#70: SNEAK INTO CUBA

By John Meils

Since it's still illegal for Americans to go to Cuba, I'll be recounting the experience of a "friend," whom I'll call "John," which also happens to be my name. John (not me) went to Cuba recently and did all of the research about how to sneak in and out of the place without getting caught and fined by Big Brother. John is a strapping, dangerously good-looking man (like me), which makes it hard for him to travel without drawing attention. So if John can do it, you can too. In fact, John thinks men who are afraid to go to Cuba might not be men at all. I tend to agree.

Before I get into specifics, a word on Cuba: It is an amazing place with cool, friendly, well-educated people who are happy as hell to see you. As an American, you are likely to be safer there than you would be walking down the street in your hometown. You see, Cubans want and need your tourist dollars, and if you're dead or freshly mugged, you can't spend them. Sadly, much of your money is likely going to find its way into Fidel Castro's pockets—or those of his brother Raúl. But some of it stands to make it to the average Cuban, with whom you'll be dealing on a day-to-day basis. Whenever possible, pay them directly.

If, despite handsome John's excellent advice, you happen to get caught returning from Cuba, don't panic. You might not even get fined and— unless you're also carrying a large bag of cocaine—you definitely won't go to jail. In truth, the U.S. law that Americans break when traveling to Cuba doesn't actually ban you from going there. It bans you from spending money there, as this is viewed as a means of aiding an enemy of the United States—a fearsome one, allegedly, given their excellent rum, really old guns, and stunningly beautiful women.

Before You Go

Cuba is not Vegas, but it's also not North Korea. You can go last-minute and still get in unscathed, but you won't find any extra limos waiting for you at the airport in Havana. You'll be lucky to get a cab. And don't bother applying for permission to go from the U.S. government unless you're a priest, an accredited journalist, or a Cuban-American. You'll not only get rejected, but you'll probably end up on every terror watch list in existence.

Most people go to Cuba via another country—usually Canada, a Caribbean island, or Mexico. According to John (who, in addition to being ruthlessly good looking, is also wicked smart), Cancún is best. There are rumors, however, that many of the Caribbean islands—like Jamaica and the Bahamas—share passenger lists from flights to and from Cuba with U.S. Customs agents. Toronto is a popular choice, but you clear customs for the United States in the Toronto airport, and it's not particularly hard to match the incoming flights with tourists who still smell of Cohibas and Mojitos.

Cancún has the benefit of being in Mexico, which doesn't play nice with U.S. Customs, and is also a favorite spot for south-of-the-border debauchery. In other words: You have plausible deniability for both your tan and your hangover. Mexico has the added advantage of not requiring U.S. citizens to have passports for entry—which means no entry stamp, making it impossible to tell where you've been when you come home. You will need a passport to enter Cuba (and to return to the U.S. via air), but the Cubans won't stamp it. Trust me (and John), they deal with jumpy Americans every day. They know the drill.

Before you go, you need to arrange for a Cuban "Tourist Card." It's like a visa and can usually be secured for around $50. These can be arranged with foreign travel agents online or taken care of in the airport in Cancún. You'll also want to bring plenty of cash to exchange for "convertible pesos," as U.S. greenbacks are no longer accepted in Cuba. Traveler's checks that are *not* drawn off U.S. banks work fine. You can also go with a "Transcard," a pre-paid debit card that is easy to set up in advance and can be used to get cash from just about any bank in Cuba.

Getting There

Two words: Cubana Air. Two more words: buckle up. There are plenty of airlines that fly into Havana, but if you're traveling through Cancún, you're probably going to end up on Cubana. This wouldn't be a problem if the airline had a good safety record and flew modern planes. They don't, on both counts. When I (and by "I," I mean John) was boarding my Cubana flight on the tarmac, I watched in horror as a bolt fell from the plane and clinked on the ground. When I tried to tell somebody, they pretended not to understand English and hustled me aboard.

Then things got really strange. The cabin filled with a mist-like fog. Once again, I asked somebody what was going on. This time I got an answer and wished I hadn't. Apparently, the plane was Russian-made and not built for hot climates, which is why they "thought" its ventilation system created mist. They assured me it was okay, though—it usually went away after takeoff. Which it did. No one else seemed as concerned as me, especially not the pilot, who left the cockpit once we were in the air and proceeded to flirt with the flight attendant while she served drinks. The door to the cockpit swung lazily open for the entire flight. The pilot returned to the controls just in time to slam the plane down onto the runway in Havana. We then taxied to the farthest point away from the terminal, where we were loaded onto a bus with no air conditioning and windows that didn't open. *Bienvenido a Cuba!*

One final thing: When you go through customs in Havana, you'll need to have a hotel arranged in advance. Or at least know the name of one. If you don't, they'll book one for you. It's a way for them to ensure that some of your tourist dollars go to the hotels, which in turn kick back to the government (i.e., the Castro brothers). As I said: *Bienvenido a Cuba!*

Getting Back

This is where most people get caught—except you, thanks to John and me. Here's the trick—and it really comes down to this: you'll have to show your passport when you return to Cancún from Havana. What you don't want them to do is stamp it, which leads to a number of uncomfortable questions when you get back to the U.S., such as: Where were you coming from when you arrived in Mexico on the same day you also left? To avoid the entry stamp in Cancún, put a folded $20-bill inside your passport and say the following words when you hand it over to Mexican immigration: *No estampilla por favor.* My guy dramatically double-stamped my immigration form, but *not* my passport. Presto! I'd officially been nowhere.

But you're not totally in the clear yet. You need to make sure you have no proof of your trip on you or in your luggage. This means no cigars, no Cuban money, no Cubana boarding passes, no Che Guevera T-shirts, no Havana tourist maps, no Cuban girlfriend on your arm, no receipts…*nada.* Get it? Everyone I know who got busted coming back from Cuba was pinched because they left something incriminating in their luggage. It's awfully hard to deny you were in Havana when you're carrying an itemized hotel receipt.

If you happen to get caught, remain calm. As I said earlier, you might not get fined. If you do, it's likely to come in the mail from the

Treasury Department's Office of Foreign Asset Control (OFAC). Now you have a decision to make. You can pay the fine, which might be as high as $10,000, or you can man up and take on the government— who many believe have no right under the First and Fifth amendments to tell their citizens where they can and cannot travel. Either way, get some legal advice. Start with the National Lawyers Guild (www. nlg.org). They have form letters you can send in response to the OFAC fine and lawyers who can help you, often for free. With a little backbone and persistence, the fine usually goes away, as the U.S. government has little interest in testing the constitutionality of its travel ban to Cuba.

Which means you'll have *another* story on top of the one about how you snuck into Cuba. Both will work wonders at the bar with that girl who you've been too afraid to talk to the last eight times you saw her. At least, John thinks so.

#71: APOLOGIZE FOR BEING UNAPOLOGETIC

By Ryan Placchetti

As a man, just going about your daily routine can rustle up the ire of the women in your life. This is not *always* the woman's fault, though. It's no secret that women and men are wired differently—like America and Europe. I mean, if you use an American toaster in Portugal, you need a power converter right? When you try to plug a woman's brain into your manly conception of logic, she might blow a fuse. Apologies are your power converters; they allow you to do what you want without destroying the women in your life. There's nothing worse than coming home from a bachelor party at three o' clock in the morning to find your soul mate smoldering in the kitchen in the midst of a meltdown.

Apologies are a delicate matter. As a man, you can't go spouting off reconciliatory language willy-nilly. That's a good way to accidentally admit that you're wrong. You've got to calculate your responses, bide your time, and strike when the proverbial iron is hot. A premature apology can make you seem weak-willed. Worse, a poorly worded apology could make you seem agreeable. There's nothing more dangerous to your manhood than self-invalidation. After all, why should she respect your masculinity if you don't? Also, keep in mind that any means of surrender you offer could erode the rights of other men in your local precinct. Taken to putting the seat down after you pee? Thanks, pal. Way to ruin it for the rest of us.

The art of apologizing to a woman is only as complicated as you make it. A relationship is karmic in nature. The more good things you do, the more bad stuff you can get away with. A diamond-studded tennis bracelet, for example, is the karmic equivalent of rescuing a busload of crippled nuns from a tidal wave. Romantic overtures bring balance and stability to a relationship. Sometimes it's as simple as writing a sappy note. Sometimes you have to buy her a Prius.

Notes on Strategy

Men often assume that an apology has to be specific to a particular offense. But just because you haven't done anything wrong doesn't mean you *don't* owe your woman an apology.

Relationships are like chess: if you intend to prevail, you need to think three or four moves ahead of your opponent. How? While it is manly to live by the seat of your pants, it is not manly to allow yourself to be controlled by the woman in your life. There's nothing worse than having to scrap a ballgame with your boys because your significant other needs so-called "quality time" (which is really code for doing what she wants to do, together). Announce that you'll be going to the game weeks in advance and start making sacrifices accordingly. Sure, there are a lot of little things you're going to miss out on while you're trying to butter up the woman you may or may not love, but you aren't going to miss out on mustard stains and drunken chanting.

The truly (un)apologetic man understands that women are retrospective animals. Their hindsight is usually crystal-clear, and they've been known to catalog missteps. However, their powers of observation can cut both ways. A woman's running tally is a perfect accumulation of your negatives *and* positives. You don't have to point out that you got her roses—she remembers. As long as she feels like she's getting equal time, you'll find it much easier to slip off with the guys and do manly things like climb rocks and drink mash whiskey out of the bottle.

Finally, a word on solidarity. Acting as a lone wolf gets you nowhere. Want to know what happens when you lay down the groundwork for getting away with future screw-ups and your pals don't? You get to screw up all by yourself. Why? Because your friends are stuck at home, scrambling to account for the disparity between their actions and yours. Remember the toilet seat? Same thing. Never make a romantic gesture without considering your buddies first.

Specific Methods of Apology

As a rule, flowers should be used sparingly. Not every woman swoons when she gets a bouquet of hyacinths and gladioluses. Modern women can be practical—and flowers are not practical. Practical women prefer diamonds.

Jewelry is a good catch-all gift. But you have to know a woman's style before you shower her with baubles. Look at the jewelry she already has, and buy her more of that type. If she has hoop earrings, buy her bigger, better hoops. If she has a heart locket, buy her a half-moon locket. If she has a Live Strong bracelet, buy her a Breast Cancer awareness bracelet. Diamonds are virtually foolproof, but should only be used as a last resort. Try cubic zirconia instead. Remember, an apology doesn't always have to stand up to long-term scrutiny; it just has to give you enough time to get the hell out of Dodge.

A well-chosen bottle of wine will often do the job. Again, it's important know her taste. Does she prefer red or a white? And how cheap is too cheap? A woman of means is probably going to expect something that runs between $40 and $80. A middle-class chick is going to fall somewhere in the $15 to $30 range. For a college girl, just buy her a box of wine, and be done with it. You shouldn't buy a high-school girl wine at all—but if you must, go with Boone's Farm. She won't know the difference.

Dinner is another good way to settle a dispute. You need to keep a few tricks in mind when crafting your ambush. Because that's what a dinner apology is—an ambush. If you've done something wrong and take her to dinner directly afterward, she'll have to deliver her grievances in public. While you can never control the level of her dissatisfaction, you can limit your exposure. Some restaurants take longer than others, so it's really a matter of how badly you screwed up. For big stuff, take her to a fancy dinner with multiple courses. For minor offenses, Wendy's will do. You can be out of a fast-food joint in under 20 minutes, long enough for her to deliver a scathing critique, yet short enough to cut off unwarranted badgering. That's fair, right?

Single Men

Let's be honest—single guys don't need much advice on the art of apologizing while being unapologetic. You can walk away at any minute. My advice for you, don't apologize at all. She'll live. If forced to apologize, try this:

"Yeah, I'm sorry. Whatever."

Saying "whatever" essentially nullifies the apologetic content of the statement. You know it, I know it, she knows it. She's going to call you on it. Then you get to say:

"What? I said I was sorry."

There's nothing she can do about it. Checkmate, *compadre*.

As a single man, you essentially can say whatever you want. You can make your apologies as hollow and false as you please. After all, what's an apology to a man and woman but a compromise between two parties to allow one party to touch the other party's private spot? Or, if you're simply tired of her, you can try something like this:

"I'm sorry you're so crazy." Guaranteed to piss her off, but who cares? You're single.

"I'm sorry, you weren't fat when I met you." Save this for someone who has seriously wronged you. The kicker to it? She doesn't have to be fat for it to be effective.

"I'm sorry, I can't go to dinner with you because I have a date tonight." He shoots, he scores.

Let your tongue unfurl, single men, for you are truly free to say and do as you wish. Emotional wreckage, be damned. Still, it wouldn't hurt to bear the rest of this article in mind, should you ever decide to take on a more serious role in a woman's life.

Apologizing to Other Men

Sometimes, you have to apologize to another dude whose priorities run counter to yours. For example, "Bring Your Daughter to Work Day" can be confusing for guys without daughters, and can lead to tension around the water cooler. Rather than apologize straight off, most men favor a direct approach. One guy attempts to assert his dominance over the other, who either accepts or rejects it. Disputes are not always resolved with fisticuffs, though it's generally agreed to be the most satisfactory conclusion.

Reason also works. For example, if your daughter is a total fox, that's probably because your wife is a babe. Take solace in that fact when swinging dicks start showing up at your front door. Conversely, if you're trying pick up another man's daughter, have respect for his domain. Try to connect with him. Have a beer, maybe discuss hunting. Note: don't actually *go* hunting at this point, as it would be very manly of him to use the opportunity to bury you deep in the woods.

Finally, try not to begrudge another man's manliness. We're all on the same team. It's inevitable that we'll occasionally find ourselves at odds with one another, but there's no shame in stepping aside every so often to make room for another guy's blaze of man glory. It's all part of the great circle of man life. Youthful cockiness, lustful conquests, and public intoxication ultimately give way to pride, discipline, and self-preservation. Ideally, only when a man strays from this circle of life must another man set him back on course. And sometimes this requires fists, broken beer bottles, and—in Southern Florida—cigar burns.

Dear Mr. Man:

The other day my girlfriend and I were getting dressed for a party and she asked me, "Honey, does this dress make me look fat?" Before I could answer, she kicked me in the balls. What's up with that?

Signed,
Ice on my Nads

Dear Ice on My Nads:

Dude, that's rough. But you deserved it. You're guilty of hesitation. To her, a one-second delay is the same as saying, "It's not the dress that makes you look fat; it is the fifty pounds of flab." In the future, I suggest anticipating questions like this one. Every morning when I wake up, I go through a 10-point checklist of questions I might expect from my loved-one during the course of the day. I practice until the answer rolls off my tongue quicker than my answer to: "Want another beer?" For the question, "Do I look fat in this dress?" I'd go with: "You look great, as always." Other examples:

Q: Do you love me?
A: Yes, I love you. I was thinking we should have a quiet dinner tonight, just the two of us.

Q: How about if we just cuddle tonight?
A: I was just thinking that, too.

Q: Are you cheating on me?
A: No, I have no interest in anyone but you, and I would never jeopardize this perfect thing we have.

Make your own list, and drill for at least 10 minutes per day. Remember—be quick, and get your response right. You don't want to stumble on, "You look great," and accidentally say, "You look fatpigfatpigfatpig." This happened to my cousin once.

Oh yeah, I forgot to ask, was she wearing pumps when she kicked you in the groin? Ouchie!

Signed,
Mr. Man

#73: SAVE YOUR STUFF

By William Tiernan

Here's a simple idea for appeasing the lady in your life who insists you trash some of your favorite items for the sake of respectability and cleanliness. We're talking about the Denver Broncos helmet lamp you've had since fourth grade; the foosball table from your college dorm room that has a few decapitated defensemen; or the framed poster of Rebecca Romijn from the *2006 All-Star Sports Illustrated Reunion* edition.

Yes, you could part with your functional and sentimental favorites, but there is an alternative. Call up your cohabitating buddies—knowing that they all have the same problem you do—and scout the most convenient storage unit facility in town. When you've found it, pool your funds and rent the biggest, baddest unit in the joint. I'm talking about the penthouse of storage units—at least 600 square feet, with strict climate control, nail-bearing walls for hanging memorabilia, multiple electrical outlets, access to outdoor seating, and anything else you need to create a bachelor pad away from home. Remember, you are splitting this puppy four ways, so this is no time to be cheap.

Once you've got your pad rented, each dude should tell his significant other that he's finally ready to rid his home of all his "junk." Then, on a designated Friday night, rent a moving truck and go from house to house loading stuff up like the Grinch on Christmas Eve. The overall mood should be somber—but mixed with a twist of chivalry, to impress upon the ladies that you are doing this for them. They may appreciate your solidarity, which earns you valuable points for cash-in later.

While the ladies are sitting around discussing how easy it was to get you guys to give up your favorite stuff, drive those said items—including the *MarsTrek* pinball machine, the 19-inch Zenith TV/VCR, the Wayne Gretzky Oilers jersey, the filthy couch only you and your dirty friends will sit on, and the dozens of other awesome things you promised to throw away—to your storage unit, stopping along the way for beer and ice (you won't need a cooler, because your buddy successfully salvaged a giant Budweiser vat that holds 83 beers from his basement). When you get to your unit, unload your stuff, arrange your bachelor pad, put the beers on ice, and pop a copy of *Predator* into the VCR.

Note: This should not turn into an every Friday- or Saturday-night activity; just visit your unit often enough to reacquaint yourself with the things you have "thrown away." When you do visit, you and your buddies should spend at least three minutes concocting a story about the way the evening was *really* spent for the sake of the ladies, so that everyone is on the same page.

THE RESOURCEFUL MAN

Go-To How-Tos for the Man Who Has Every Situation Covered

#74: Fix Any Modern Device

By R. Andrew Lamonica

An important note about modern devices: just because they're not working doesn't mean they're broken. So, before your wife or girlfriend calls your neighbor (who might have a bigger and better set of tools than you), run through this simple checklist.

1. Is it turned on?

The first rule of modern devices is that they invariably have an "on" state and an "off" state. Familiarize yourself with the method of transitioning between the two. Many devices can be fixed simply by performing such a transition. When attempting to fix a device with this approach, take your time. Give the device a chance to settle into the selected state before toggling back. Switching rapidly between on and off rarely works, and it makes you look like you don't know what you're doing.

2. Is it plugged in?

If it's more complicated than a bottle-opener, it probably requires electricity to function. Make sure plenty of electricity is available to the broken device. This may require winding a spring, changing batteries, checking the state of wall outlets and power strips, or even leaving something to recharge overnight. Adding power might not fix what ails the device, but you can bet that the opposite prevents it from functioning, even if that's not the full extent of the problem.

3. What is the broken device trying to tell me?

Most devices—from VCRs to computers to vacuum cleaners—have error indicators. An indicator may be as cryptic as a blinking light, or as blatant as a "Cyan Toner Cartridge Empty" message. If the error message is clear, respond to its implied instructions. If the error message is confusing, type it into Google to see how others have solved the problem.

4. Who do I know who is smarter than me?

It's hard to find an honest professional to fix your device (versus selling you a new one). However, there are people in the world who know more about your broken device than you do. Swallow your pride, and invite one of them over for a beer. Once he has plugged your television into an outlet that actually works, offer him the entire six-pack and turn on the football game. If a 10-year-old fixes your device, get him a cold lemonade and challenge him to a game of UNO; if he's troubleshooting at age 10, he's at risk of becoming a lifelong geek and needs immediate socialization.

#75: SPLINT A FRACTURE WITH A SPATULA AND A ROLL OF DUCT TAPE

#76: CHOOSE A NEW CAREER

By John Meils

So the acting thing didn't work out. Your cushy Wall Street job is gone. You finally outgrew the boy band. So what? Starting over means doing what you really want. That's what everyone says, anyway. Then they go and do the same old thing in a different way, and get paid less for it. But not you—not this time. You're going to live the dream. You're going to combine your passions with your livelihood. You're going to be the envy of everyone you know because you said: "Not me! Not this time! I'm going to become rich and famous and sleep with beautiful women! And I don't care if it's just because I'm rich! I'm okay with that! Because I'll be doing something I love!"

By "something you love," I'm referring to the same three things all men love: drinking beer, having sex, and watching TV. Too often, we men fail to combine our favorite pastimes with our careers because we're afraid. Of what, you ask? Our bills, our reputations, our families? Maybe. Or are we afraid of being happy, which is exactly what happens when you make a living by drinking beer, having sex, or watching TV?

Because it can happen. There are loads of careers that allow you to get paid for drinking beer, having sex, or watching TV. Think I'm crazy? I am. Crazy like a fox who drinks beer, has sex, and watches TV all the time! What follows is a small selection of jobs that allow you to live the dream. There are myriad others. Consider this list as a glimpse— the first beer from the six-pack, if you will:

Drinking Beer

Naturally, having sex should come first. It's better than drinking beer. If you think it's not, you're either having way too much sex or far too little—or maybe you're just not doing it right. Either way, I put beer first because it's always there for men. It won't divorce or dump us, and we can still drink it when the power goes out and the TV doesn't work. Beer comes in near-limitless flavors and packages too. You can have light beer, dark beer, lager, stout, pale ale, bitter, microbrews, warm beer, cold beer, keg beer…administered through a bottle, sipped through a growler, poured down your throat with a funnel, or chugged from a Solo cup.

Most importantly, beer brings men together. "Want a beer?" is practically a greeting. The response—"Don't ya think it's a little early?"—is a joke that never gets old (because really, is it ever too early for a beer? I think not.). What I'm trying to convey is the inherent joy that beer brings into the lives of men. You can grab a bigger share of that joy by getting one of the following jobs:

Brewmaster: This is the Merlin of beer jobs. When you make beer for a living, you aren't merely crafting an alcoholic beverage; you're bottling bliss. Ever met a surly, depressed brewmaster? I haven't. They are joyous people, because doing their job well means constantly tasting their product and that of the competition. That's right, *not* drinking beer all day would be grounds for dismissal. Now for the hard part—becoming a professional beer maker. My suggestion is to start at the bottom. Get thee to a brewery, and offer to sweep the floors for free until a better position opens up. They'll admire your dedication, and—at the very least—should pay you with free beer. From there, the sky's the limit.

Beer Delivery Guy: Who doesn't love the beer guy? He's the Santa Claus of hops, driving around in a sleigh designed to carry hundreds of cases of sudsy goodness, which he doles out to those

naughty *and* nice. The pay isn't great, but think of the job satisfaction, of the smiles you bring whenever you roll a fully stacked hand truck into a new store. Insurance salesmen can only *dream* of enjoying that kind of love on a daily basis. And, frankly, it's not a terribly hard job to get. You'll probably have to be the second guy on the truck for a while, but soon enough, that beer rig will be all yours.

Bum: I prefer to call them "beer monks," because it's a lifestyle choice. Being a bum isn't for everybody, but for those who make the leap into the rarified beer-only diet…well, how can you knock that type of spiritual dedication? Another bonus is that you don't have to pay for beer ever again. Even the worst panhandler can score enough dough for a few beers a day. You'll likely have to lower your brand standards (and sleep on hot vents in winter), but good things require sacrifice. Best of all, there's absolutely no training necessary to become a bum. You can start right away.

Having Sex

The practice of making money off sex gets a bad rap. Admittedly, there's an unseemly side to the business, but you don't have to jump in with both feet right away. And, hey, maybe having sex for a living isn't for you. Maybe you don't like sex, or worry that having it all the time will ruin it for you (it won't, FYI). There's still beer and TV, after all.

However, for certain bold men, having sex for a living is the perfect marriage of hobby and commerce. It comes with baggage, clearly, but the upside is that you'll be too busy getting laid to worry about what other people think.

Porn-Site Entrepreneur: I can't say for sure, but this has got to be the easiest way to get rich by having sex. I mean, there are trillions of porn sites out there. How hard could it be? Sure, you'll probably have to fudge the truth about what you do around your buddy's girlfriend, and you definitely won't be able to tell your grandmother how you paid for your new Mercedes. But you'll be making so much money, it won't matter. Start-up costs would seem low as well. All you need is a digital camera, a website (which you can build yourself), and your neighbor's wife.

Boy Toy: This is one of those careers that you stumble upon in your youth. Unfortunately, it doesn't last long. It's like being a running back in the NFL: you've only got about six to eight years before the younger, stronger guys elbow you out of the starting job. But those six to eight years are the ones you talk about for the rest of your life. To get the job, it helps to have a lot of energy, the ability to take orders, and an inborn hatred of paying for anything yourself (seriously, are those the same two twenties in your wallet since last Christmas?). Nobody likes a boy toy who won't be kept.

Man Whore: For the hardcore only. The trick is to be able to pick and choose your clients. But for the serious man whore, this shouldn't matter. You're in it for the sex and the glory of making a living at it. The world "no" isn't part of your vocabulary. You might have to hide your true identity (except from other man whores, who will become your only friends), but that's part of the life you've chosen. Rock on, man whore. You, sir, are getting it done while getting it on.

Watching TV

For some, especially the aged (and wise) man, watching TV for a living is the Holy Grail. This is because it not only rocks on its own, but can be easily combined with drinking beer and even having sex. And let's face it, there might be hundreds of different kinds of beer out there, but there are thousands of channels on TV, and more being added every day. Also, you don't have to do *anything* while watching TV. Sometimes, I get so entranced I forget to breathe, which leads to sleep, another excellent man-activity that can be combined with TV.

Since there are relatively few jobs that involve simply watching TV all the time, the occupations I suggest *indirectly* allow you to do it for a living. That said, I've tried to focus on the important part, which is non-stop TV viewing for money.

Cable Guy: Thanks to Hollywood and a few bad seeds, being a cable guy doesn't have the cachet it deserves. Before I get to free cable, let's talk about the uniforms. How awesome are they? And you don't have to mess up (or regularly clean) your good clothes. Also, being a cable guy can sometimes be combined with having sex, if you're particularly lucky and the uniform fits you really well. Oh, and you get to not only watch TV all day; you get paid to bring it to others. So you've got the whole karmic thing going for you. And you can hook up all of your friends with free cable, including the sex channels. Which basically makes you Robin Hood.

Bookie: A classically overlooked profession. So you take bets for a living? How is that different from Wall Street? At least when your clients don't pay up, you have some recourse besides begging the government for help. If all the CEOs of those failed investment banks were publicly knee-capped, I think it's safe to wager that they wouldn't make so many risky bets next time. Besides the respect and fear that comes with the job, you're really just watching TV all the time. Better still, you're watching sports on TV, and your livelihood is dramatically tied to the outcome of each game. That's living. And don't forget that you can (and probably should) drink beer while doing your job.

Writer: The big joke about writers is that they work for an hour or two each day, and spend the rest of their time watching TV. As a writer, I'm here to tell that it's absolutely true. I bet you Stephen King watches at least 10 hours of TV a day. And you get access to daytime

TV, which is definitely bitchy and strange and cloying, but often surprisingly better than nighttime TV. Also, you're a writer, which is a (mostly) respected profession, and one where you're expected to be a drunk, so the beer part is covered. The downside is the money, which is only there for Stephen King. No one else makes a dime.

Conclusion

The preceding list was meant to be as inspirational as it was practical. In my experience, if you're not focused on living the beer-drinking, sex-having, TV-watching dream, it'll never happen. However, if you're both committed and creative, there are literally hundreds of potential "man-propriate" careers out there. The ones listed above are just the low-hanging fruit. So get thinking, men. You've got a new career to choose. Still not sure? Maybe you should crack open a beer, turn on the TV, and give your lady a call as you ponder the possibilities.

#77: CHANGE A TIRE IN UNDER FOUR SECONDS WITHOUT THE HELP OF AN AIR GUN

#78: GRACEFULLY LOSE TO YOUR BOSS IN GOLF

#79: Cook One Thing Well

By Karen Gibson

Do you consider the ability to spell "kitchen" your main culinary talent? Do you need an instruction manual to boil an egg? If you're subsisting on Hungry Man dinners and take-out Chinese, you're short-changing yourself. Whether it's your Italian grandmother's spaghetti sauce from scratch or leg of lamb, every man should be able to put something on the table with pride. Here are the tips to do just that:

1. Tell a story. Whatever recipe or dish you decide to go with, make sure it has a great story behind it. Nothing's better than listening to a guy tell you how this spaghetti sauce has been handed down through generations in his family, or how steak reminds him of cooking with his dad. Get the picture? Now she understands your inner workings, *and* she thinks you're adorable.

2. It's the result that counts. Your meal doesn't have to have over 20 ingredients or be listed on Emeril's "hardest things to cook" list. It just has to taste phenomenal and exhibit great presentation. Use the freshest herbs and ingredients you can find. Meals that come out of a box taste like they came out of a box.

3. Make it pretty. As any chef will tell you, presentation is almost as important as the meal itself. There's no need to come up with island-theme tablescapes, but make your meal attractive to all of the senses. Let the meal decorate the plate, and invite the recipient to smell and taste it as it cooks.

4. What's for dinner? Don't have a family recipe that you want to try? Not a fan of the Food Network? Not to fret. What is your favorite thing to eat? Who makes it? If you answered, say, "meatloaf made by mom"…well, you know where you need to go to get the recipe and tips. If you answered "a well-cooked steak from Morton's," do some research. Hit the Internet for cooking tips for different cuts of beef, the best herbs and seasonings, and how to cook rare, medium, and well-done to perfection

5. Practice makes perfect. Practice preparing your "signature" meal several times before you present it to anyone else. I remember getting a "slap yo' mama" apple-pie recipe from an elderly neighbor. She could only provide estimates, at best, for how much of each ingredient to use and how long to cook it. It took seven pies until I got it right. Thank goodness I didn't decide to show up to a family reunion with that first disastrous pie! Impress yourself with your meal first, then serve it up to whomever you wish to astonish.

Good luck—and when you have it down, give me a call!

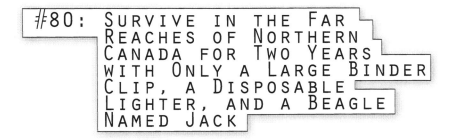

#80: SURVIVE IN THE FAR REACHES OF NORTHERN CANADA FOR TWO YEARS WITH ONLY A LARGE BINDER CLIP, A DISPOSABLE LIGHTER, AND A BEAGLE NAMED JACK

#81: Buy a Used Car without Losing Your Shirt

By Vanessa Cobb

When you buy a car from a private sale, you have to live with it, like it or not. So *caveat emptor*—and for those of us who never studied Latin, buyer beware.

A used-car dealer may tempt you with glittering chrome, but he probably knows the quickest way into your pocket and a thousand ways to slip out of town in a hurry. All the same, that doesn't make a private sale a walk in the park. When you do find the car of your dreams, here's how you can avoid getting stuck with a lemon, oil the cogs of the deal, and score points with your girlfriend—all in one profitable maneuver.

Let's face it, you're reading this guide so you can look like a pro. Follow these easy steps, and you'll have the previous owner in the palm of your hand, and your date purring in minutes.

1. Arm Yourself at Home First

Arm yourself with information. Before you touch that vehicle, you need to know what it's worth. Once you know the make, model, year, and mileage, check the Kelley Blue Book and shoot for up to 10% less.

That's if it's in mint condition. Deduct repair costs for anything that isn't up to scratch.

Come prepared with a heap of intelligent questions. How long have you had the car? Has it ever been in an accident? When was it last serviced? What kind of problems have you had?

Make a daylight appointment to view the car, and pray for good weather.

2. The Dress Rehearsal

Leave your best chinos in the closet, and dig out a pair of last year's Levi's. Wear a loose button-down shirt over a spotless tank top. Read on to find out why!

Take a flashlight with you—or, better still, ask to borrow one from your girlfriend. You need to involve her as much as possible.

Memorize and conceal these instructions. A good actor learns the script and doesn't blow his cover with a crib sheet.

If the funds are there, visit the bank and withdraw enough to cover your top price. Ask your girlfriend to stash $50 in her purse, in case you need it.

3. The First Encounter

Be courteous. Nothing displays confidence and builds trust more quickly than behaving like a gentleman right from the start.

Once the greeting is over, ask your questions. Take all the answers with a grain of salt. Keep the poker face fixed, though, and resist the urge to laugh out loud; blatant distrust is unattractive. Ask to see all the records—including repair documents—and say goodbye if it says 'salvage' on the title.

As the owner begins his pitch, slowly unbutton your shirt, take it off, and hand it to your lady. This has two valuable benefits: first, it shows you're not going to take his word for anything, and second, it makes your girl part of the team. Women love that.

4. The Inspection

Get straight to the ground, and start looking around the underside by flashlight. This is likely to make the vendor uncomfortable, but here's what you're looking for:

Rust. Check the chassis, the jack point, and the exhaust. Look out for any holes, too.

Leaking oil. Check everywhere, but take a close look inside the front wheels where they connect with the axle. The last thing you want is evidence of a broken CV joint. This kind of repair is seldom permanent and could mean endless upkeep.

Bulges in the inner tire walls. You don't want a blow-out on the freeway.

Under-sealing starting to peel. Another early warning signal.

Move about 20 feet from the front of the car, and check to see that the fender is parallel with the ground.

Lean on each corner of the car, and count how many times it bounces when you let go. If it jumps more than twice, it needs new shock absorbers.

Examine the tread on the tires for life expectancy and for signs of cracking in the tire wall.

Now it's time to open the hood. Watch the owner's body language; this should be the most nerve-wracking part for the seller. We know you're not a mechanic, but he doesn't. All

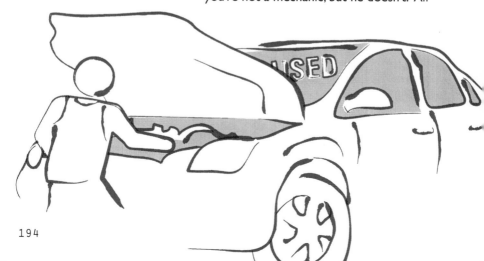

you're looking for is clean engine oil to indicate a recent service, but take your time and raise your eyes a little if you're enjoying the drama.

Ask your girl to watch the front wheels while you turn the steering wheel slowly. Have her let you know when she sees them move; it shouldn't take more than about an inch and a half of turning. Ask her to check all the lights too.

5. The Test Drive

Start the engine, but have your date wait beside the car for a moment. You want to hear smooth idling, and she needs to see that any blue smoke from the exhaust dissipates quickly.

Get out of the car, and open the front passenger door for your friend. Ask the owner if he wants to join you to see how it handles. If he leaves you to it, great—you can have that private exchange she's dying for; but if he's in the back, use it to your advantage. Make chit-chat about the car to find out how he's been driving it. A good way is to ask about his most memorable journeys.

Move through all the gears, listening carefully for a smooth transition. Make sure there are no shudders and bangs from the engine at 30 miles per hour. Check all of the electronics, including windshield washers and wipers, rear-window defroster, and even the light in the glove box.

Find a safe spot to test the brakes. Take it up to 40 miles per hour, and hit the brakes like you mean it. As the vehicle slows, take your hands an inch away from the wheel, and check to make sure it doesn't pull to the left. If anything, a very slight pull away from oncoming traffic is fine.

6. The Show Down

If you think it's worth buying, ask the lady if she likes it. Estimate the cost of all of the repairs you suspect are needed and mentally factor them into your highest offer. If you can't settle for less than this price, be ready to walk away.

Turn to the seller and ask: "So what do you want for it?" Whatever he answers, adopt your best George Clooney smile, and shake your head while making friendly eye contact. At this point, the first one to speak loses, so wait before you hit him with a counter offer.

Reply with a winning line: "We weren't looking to pay that much." She's smiling at the "we," while he's contemplating the "pay."

Now he's itching to know more. Justify your offer point by point before you make a bid. Nod politely to his response.

Finally, open your wallet and flick the notes. "Let's see if we can do this a little more simply," you say. "If we can settle on "[X]," I think we could all save ourselves some time." Take out the cash and say, "Hmm. Fifty dollars short. Honey, would you mind?" As she hands you the extra notes, he'll be salivating at the sight of it—and totally numbed by your nerve.

When you've bought the car, pick up a small bouquet of flowers for your lovely assistant to let her know you couldn't have managed such a great deal without her help. Women know that flowers usually mean you've done something bad, so grab this unique chance to show her you're a more evolved kind of guy.

#82: ROLL A JOINT

By Curtis Manchester

Whether you're backpacking through Europe, heading to the beach, or hanging out on the couch, rolling a primo doob— err, I mean, a primo *hand-rolled cigarette* is an essential piece of know-how. It might take a little while to learn, but once you've gained some mastery of these stoner arts-and-crafts, there's no end to the accolades you'll receive as the reigning jointmaster.

Practice this step-by-step technique a few dozen times. Don't worry if you mess up at first; rolling a cone is a finesse job, and the first few attempts never go as planned. Fire up an episode of *Aqua Teen Hunger Force,* and in no time you'll be asking your buddies, "What were we just talking about?"

1. Gather your green. Grab your stash (of tobacco) and start breaking up the buds. Pick the leaves off the stems and shred them a bit with your fingers. For your first time, try to gather a small pile of shavings—about the diameter of a silver dollar. Once you're more practiced, feel free to graduate to larger mounds of smoke.

2. Make a filter. Any schmo with some schwag and a piece of paper can twist up a serviceable joint. But to create a truly sophisticated and impressive cone, you'll need a filter. To make one, rip a small rectangle off the end of a business card or hard pack of cigarettes. Any thick paper stock will do. You want the rectangle to be about one inch long by a half inch wide. Start at the short end and roll

it tight, like a miniature carpet or a sleeping bag. Work it between your thumb and middle finger until a very tight spiral is formed and it doesn't immediately unravel when you let go. Set this filter aside.

3. Choose your rolling paper. Try to get Smoking brand papers, or a pack of thin Rizlas; the crease runs lengthways down the center. A good rolling paper is essential to the process.

4. Make your bed. Hold the paper lengthwise, with the strip of glue running horizontally on the edge farthest from your body. Place your filter in the crease on the right side of the paper and hold it there with your right hand. Lightly pinching the filter and the paper together with just your right fingers, create a nice "V" crease in the paper. This maneuver leaves your left hand free to work. Sprinkle your shredded leaves into the crease of the paper. Spread it evenly, using your fingertip to make sure there's ample greenage against the filter.

5. Get it rolling. Keeping the paper level, use the thumb and first two fingers of each hand to begin rolling the tobacco into a cylindrical mass. Keep rolling the paper like this, pretending that you're feeling some nice fabric. Roll it gently until the cylinder is even.

6. The curl. Here's the tricky part. Ninety-four percent of all joints are ruined in this phase (statistics may not be accurate). When the paper is low on the side closest to you, and you can see a hint of the leaves in the center of your paper peeking out, very carefully curl the bottom right edge—using your right thumb—over and behind the filter on the right side of your joint. Make this curl as tight as possible against the filter; that's what holds this whole thing together. If you can get a tight curl, gently lick the glue from end to end, and immediately keep rolling the joint into that glue, lightly smoothing the glue-seam with your finger as you get to the end. You should be able to hold the whole thing upright by the filter. Keep trying until you either master the curl or rip the paper and have to start over.

7. Pack it up, pack it in. Grip the paper between thumb and forefinger at the loose excess at the left, non-filter end of the joint. Swing it back and forth a few times like you're fanning yourself. Here, you're trying to push the loose leaves into a nicely packed mass further down toward the filter. You can open up the loose top end and add back the stuff that might've fallen out during the rolling process. You can also use the eraser end of a pencil to pack it in. Be careful not to rip the paper here, though. The other six percent of all joints are ruined in this phase.

8. Seal the chamber. Twist off the excess paper at the top end. If the joint body feels loose, you can lightly lick the whole thing, gently wind it tighter, then very quickly fan the length of it with a lighter flame.

9. Smoke up. Light the twisted end (not the filter end, genius), and let it burn off. The rest should be obvious, but make sure the joint is lit evenly around the whole circumference of the fat end, so that it burns evenly the whole way down. If it starts to canoe (in which one side burns much faster than the other), lightly lick your finger and wet the paper along the side where it's burning faster. This should even it out.

10. Enjoy. Puff, puff, pass. Feel free to relax. The beauty of these cone joints is that they burn a bit slower and don't go out as often, so you can be more leisurely about your process.

11. Turn on some Pink Floyd and marvel at your handiwork.

Dear Mr. Man:

I don't know a thing about gadgets or tools. I don't know which way to turn a screwdriver, and I'm really scared of electricity. Lately, my wife has been asking our neighbor, Randy, to fix stuff. He's a contractor with silky blonde hair and a big tool box. When he struts in, I get pushed into a corner with my iced tea. The only thing I can do around the house is open a jam jar. I hit it on the table, then give it a twist. For the sake of my manliness, please tell me how to fix things.

Signed,
Tool Impaired

Dear Tool Impaired,

Everything you need to know about fixing things can be learned from that jam jar. Solving most household problems is a two-step process. First, you hit it. Then you add power. It's exactly what you do with the jam jar: You hit it on the table, and then give it a good turn—also known as "hand power."

But what about the TV remote? You've pointed it at the TV from 23 different angles, and you're still stuck watching the PBS special on the origins of yodeling. Here's how you fix it: Hit the remote on the table. No go? Add power: A new battery.

You can do the exact same thing with flashlights, electric pencil sharpeners, and your wife's dildo. Bigger items like coffeemakers, TVs, and refrigerators should be struck with an open hand, or kicked with an adequately shod foot. And remember: big things require big power. Your fridge doesn't spit ice cubes and chill milk on a couple of double-A's. The fridge's power comes from the wall, so check the plug. Lastly, if your efforts don't work, don't stand there looking defeated and puzzled, and definitely don't get Randy. Sigh and say, "Probably a fuse." Then call a real pro.

Signed,
Mr. Man

P.S. While you've been reading this, that Randy guy with the big tool box has been fantasizing about your beautiful wife. Get a move on, my friend.

#84: Reprogram an X-Box to Detect the Presence of the Undead

#85: Iron a Suit

#86: KILL A RAT

By William Tiernan

The Nature of the Rat

There are several things to understand about rats before trying to kill one.

1. They like cat food.

2. They are social creatures—which is to say they get along well with each other and other animals, particularly cats. They despise humans.

3. Sixty-five percent of household rats are discovered in the bathtub. For instance, you're getting ready to plop your daughter in the tub and you realize that the eight-inch-long gray rodent with the leathery tail is not one of her plastic bath toys. Nor is it Nicodemus from *Mrs. Frisby and the Rats of Nimh*.

4. Rats are excellent swimmers—and they aren't bothered by rat poison, at least not the stuff purchased from Wal-Mart. Supposedly, cedar and pine oil are toxic to rats, but from my experience, they actually enjoy having this stuff sprayed on them. So, if and when you do find a rat in your bathtub, and you try to drown it while spraying it with "poison," the most likely result is a rat seemingly enjoying a day at the beach, for which you just provided the 45 SPF sunblock.

5. Rat teeth are strong enough to nibble through lead piping, brick, and concrete. Therefore, unless you are doing well enough for

yourself to have a pool (and thus, have one of those leaf scoopers you can use to extract the rat from your tub), don't get anywhere near the thing. If you do have such a scooper, stop reading this, simply scoop up the rat, and dump him over the fence and into your neighbor's pool.

6. Traditional rat traps don't kill rats. These traps are intended to break the backs of small rodents. Rats aren't small. You could eat a three-course meal off the backside of a healthy-sized rat. Throwing a trap in your bathtub is not going to get it done; you've now simply provided the rat with an inner tube.

In light of all this advice, if you do discover a rat in your bathtub and you don't want a new pet, a logical plan would be to: (a) call an exterminator; or (b) locate your shotgun, and pump the sucker full of ammo (yes, guns can kill rats). But both plans have the same flaw: by the time the exterminator shows up, or by the time you've retrieved your shotgun, the rat will have escaped the bathtub. Incidentally, I can't say for sure how or why rats get into bathtubs, considering that they don't jump well and they can't climb slick surfaces like porcelain. Nevertheless, they get in all the same—and if the fuckers can get in, they sure as hell can get out. Even if you keep the shotgun in your bathroom closet next to your Speed Stick, you may miss the rat and put a hole through your tub. Or you may blow your damn foot off. Also, shooting a contained rat is like hunting deer trapped in cages, or fishing in stocked ponds; it's simply unsportsmanlike.

If you don't dispose of the rat immediately, you need a plan to exterminate the thing at a later time. The plan should be intelligent and sporting, and offer some serious delayed gratification, akin to the situation in which Darth Vadar let Luke and his rebel friends escape the Death Star at the end of *Star Wars*, knowing the real fun had yet to begin. That way, you might be able to sell the plan to your girlfriend, who is pissed that you didn't man up and kill the thing immediately in the tub. On the other hand, if you're looking for a way to get your girlfriend to move out, simply set "Fluffy" up in front of the television in a video rocker, and pop in *The Dark Crystal*.

Okay, now for the intelligent, sporting, delayed gratification plan for killing the rat.

1. After leaving the rat to "escape" your bathtub, block access to all your closets. Rats can climb and descend stairs, and closets are their prime nesting and hiding place—given that they're dark and roomy, with a bunch of stuff to hide under and gnaw on. With your closets secure, the rat has two hiding options: If it entered your home from within your walls, it can return the same way, probably through a ground-level heating vent; or it can hide under a piece of furniture that offers protection, like a couch. Whichever it favors, this item should serve as its future trap.

2. Secure a cat. Yes, a cat. If you live with a woman, you might also be living with a cat; if you live by yourself, you hopefully don't own a cat, so you need to get one. I recommend borrowing a neighbor's feline for a few weeks; it's going to be a temporary stay, and like I said, rats and cats get along like Barry Bonds and steroids.

3. Buy a bunch of wet cat food. Not that Fancy Feast stuff, but the big, cheap, large cans of Nine Lives or something similar. Be sure to buy in variety, and don't get the gourmet stuff. Go with the staples: Chicken, beef, cod, liver, and so on.

4. Locate several plastic bowls—one for each variety of cat food—and label accordingly. Don't use paper plates; the rat will eat them, and possibly upset your plan. He also may eat the plastic bowls, but more slowly.

An obvious question at this point is: Why would you feed a rodent that you want to dispose of? Good question, so let's move on.

5. Before going to sleep that first night of the rat's appearance, set up the buffet. Start with helpings of chicken, liver, cod, whitefish, and

beef chunks. Be sure your buffet includes the cat's favorite dish, and remember to label your bowls. Now, here's where the social nature of the rat comes into play. If the rat is the only animal in the house, and you leave some food out for him, he won't leave his hiding place for fear of a trap; but, when he sees the cat belly up to the buffet, he's going along for the ride. No one likes to eat alone; the cat and rat will welcome each other's company—as long as there's enough food to go around.

6. In the morning, study the bowls carefully. By excluding the bowl the cat ate from (and assuming its appetite didn't double overnight), you can determine the rat's cat food preference. The rest is easy.

7. For the next week to ten days, lay out four to five bowls of the rat's favorite cat food each night, and let the sucker chow down, buffet-style.

8. While the rat is fattening, decide on the instrument of death. I suggest something that allows sufficient distance between you and the rat, like a bat, a hockey stick, or—better yet—a golf club with a graphite shaft to maximize swing speed. A club with an oversized titanium head is a bonus. If you have such a club but suck at golf, go to the driving range to practice.

9. Wait for the rat to get stuck on its way into hiding. With an unlimited supply of food, the rat is going to expand several waist

sizes in a week. Pretty soon, that heating vent or crawl space under the couch is going to be a tight squeeze for the rat. He won't notice, though, because he'll be too high on a steady diet of Fisherman's Catch.

10. Then, when you least expect it—when you've attached yourself to the couch for some Saturday college football, for example—you hear it: the squealing of the rat. Rats don't have tonsils, which makes their howling sound not of this world. It's heinous, and when you hear it, you know the rat is trapped.

11. There's no need to rush at this point. Finish your beer, smoke a cigar, go take a dump; the rat is not going anywhere. His ass has gotten so big that it has developed its own weather pattern, and that ass is sticking out from either the heating vent or the couch. If you're a real bastard, you may want to rest your beer on its backside—or a whole six pack, if you're watching *Braveheart*. If not, simply retrieve your bashing instrument of choice and exterminate the beast. If you have a sworn enemy who owes you money, stick the rat in his mailbox as a friendly warning.

#87: Chase a Villain across the Roof of a Moving Train

#88: Write a Truly Amazing Cover Letter

#89: Keep Your Cool in Traffic

By Nancy S. Mure

Do you go from zero to beast in seconds when faced with a little bumper-to-bumper traffic? If roadway congestion is your kryptonite, don't despair. With a little discipline, and some tried-and-true techniques, you'll conquer your road rage and live a happier, more peaceful life on the highway.

You've been there—stuck in a horrendous traffic jam, cursing yourself for your bad timing, and wishing you knew how to get around it. It's time for you to learn how to cope. Gentlemen, I humbly offer you a lifeline for working out your issues:

Be negative. If you've vowed to have a positive outlook in life, now is not the time to start. Instead, expect the worst, and factor traffic into your ride. Tell yourself, "There will be traffic today—lots and lots of it. I will be stuck for hours!" If you plan for the worst, anything you encounter along the way will be better than expected.

Where's the sport in this? Like any sport, dealing with traffic requires strategy and a good offense. To ready yourself for being stuck, fill up the gas tank, create a play list (anything that calms the savage beast works), grab a newspaper, some magazines—and a bag of chewy Swedish fish for those teeth-clenching moments. Then open up the sunroof and hit the road. If you hit traffic, just settle in and enjoy yourself.

Procrastination doesn't prolong life. Let's face it: if you had a choice between mowing the lawn and having a beer with your buddies, there'd be no contest. Assuming you absolutely need to be somewhere, and you've accepted the inevitable existence of traffic, the drudgery of getting on the road is equivalent to mowing the lawn, and that's a major buzz kill. Leaving earlier can make all the difference, so weigh your options. Do you really need to catch another inning or play one more round of *Guitar Hero,* or can you hit the road right now? My suggestion? Suck it up, and buy an extra pack of Swedish Fish!

Roger, over, and out! Commission a co-pilot. At the end of the day, everyone in the car has a responsibility for the backlash of a bad ride. If you give your riders a heads-up that you're a psycho in traffic, chances are they'll help to silence the voices and come up with strategies to save you—and themselves. Enlist your passengers to help you count license plates or think of every adjective that starts with the letter "S."

Talk dirty to me. As long as you haven't already reached your boiling point, the thought of sex may be an excellent distraction. Assuming you're sitting in traffic with your significant other, have your prisoner—er, passenger—read something sassy to you. *Cosmo* and *Playboy* have some terrific articles! Of course, this strategy depends on who's riding shotgun. Your wife or girlfriend will probably be better at this than your Uncle Moe.

Let go, my ego! Traffic doesn't happen to *you.* If it did, you wouldn't be sitting in it, would you? Traffic happens to hundreds of people at once, so don't take it personally. Look around. Realizing you're not the only one stuck gets you out of your head into reality. Maybe you'll even have a little sympathy for the woman next to you—you know, the one heaving through her contractions? She needs to get somewhere, just like you!

If you can't handle it, avoid it. Several reasonably priced portable GPS devices cater to Neanderthals who freak in traffic. Liberate yourself from clogged highways and ghastly backups with live traffic updates and alternatives to circumvent a pile-up. If this option is too pricey, use your cell phone. There are plenty of free traffic-busting 800 numbers available locally that give alternative routes—just Google 'em.

Never put off the good things. You're a manly man, and traffic isn't bigger than you. Letting traffic keep you from family events, anniversaries, birthday celebrations, and generally having a good time isn't cool—period.

Take no prisoners! Accept jam ups as a part of life. Add it to the list of things we have to do: Die, pay taxes, and sit in traffic. When it's over, let it go. *Guitar Hero,* anyone?

#90: SAVE SOMEONE'S LIFE USING THE HEIMLICH MANUEVER

#91: Wow a First Date on a Dime

By Tahra Seplowin

ace it, guys: The courting game is biased toward men willing to spend money. As the saying goes, you never get a second chance to make a first impression. In the world of first dates, women appreciate things like nice dinners, good wine, the theater, and flowers. Sure, your wallet may be lighter than it was at the beginning of a date (unless you're wearing out the magnetic strip on your plastic), but dropping a decent amount of money shows us you're interested and proves you have a decent job—or a trust fund.

Still, the majority of women forgive a lack of money spent on a first date if you substitute thoughtfulness and creativity. Don't wince. It's not that hard to think of something inexpensive (or free) to do instead of going out to a nice restaurant or lounge. You don't have to do a weekend getaway or a road trip that guzzles more gas than a SUV-driving suburban soccer mom. With a bit of research, planning, and romance, you'll get top marks without the red numbers on your bank statement.

The First Date

You're interested, you want to make a good first impression, but you're not yet sure if she's worth 100 bucks. Here are some first-date options.

Wining and Dining

For a casual atmosphere, take her on a picnic. Bread, bagels, cheese, ham, water, and wine are the staples of a quality picnic. (Of course, don't forget the blanket and fold-out chairs.) Parks are good, but not dog parks; she doesn't want to sit in poop. Take her somewhere quiet and clean. Extra points for a good view.

If you want to take her out, an inexpensive restaurant is fine. "Dives" can have the best food in town, and she is likely to appreciate one that holds sentimental value for you. A few trips down memory lane offer her a "taste" for your personality—and if you know the joint, she can count on you to order the best "off-the-menu" items along with the perfect house beer or wine.

Or take her to the supermarket, and have her pick out ingredients for the best home-cooked meal of her life. She can enjoy a nice glass of wine as you navigate your kitchen like Iron Chef. Choose this dining option only if you can deliver the goods; if you can't turn on the oven—or if your place is a mess—take her out.

Wining and dining notes: eat, drink, and be merry, but don't booze it up. Getting too drunk, too fast is a sure way to turn a promising first date into an only date.

Entertainment

To avoid the potential awkward silences of dinner, choose an active, entertaining first date. Let other people do the talking by going to a movie. Or take in a performance at a local college or museum. Colleges put on quality, inexpensive shows (so you won't have to spend an entire paycheck on two tickets for a Broadway musical), and museums are goldmines of free (yes, free) entertainment. If she's into sports, take her to the driving range, go to the batting cage, or play pool.

Gifts

It's a first date, so don't sweat it. If there's a spontaneous, spur of the moment opportunity during the date to get her a simple gift guaranteed to make her smile, go for it.

Payment

None of these first dates should set you back more than $30. Because of the low price tag, we expect you to pay. Waffling on this matter makes you seem like a cheap bastard, which doesn't bode well for a second date. Don't forget that your date isn't the only one judging you. Ten of her friends—minimum—are waiting to get a full report. If you asked her to split the cost of the popcorn and soda at the movies, her friends will make sure she never calls you again, no matter how sparkling your personality happens to be.

The Blind Date

So your mom set you up with her old college roommate's best friend's co-worker's daughter, who just moved into town. You can't say no to Mom, but you should treat a first date like a hurricane: Be prepared. First, make sure Mom understands that she will be held personally responsible for anything that goes wrong. Second, devise a well-coordinated escape plan with a reliable friend. Try the old "If I call and ring twice, you call back in five minutes and pretend you're my dying grandmother" standby. Finally, think of your date like an accordion. It starts out short, but once the music kicks in, you can open it up and let it wail. Ask your blind date to meet you for one drink. If she ends up laughing at your joke about the sailor and the bighorn sheep, suggest a leisurely dinner or a movie. If you don't hit it off, don't sweat it. Pay for her mojito, and go meet up with your buddies at the bar across the street.

#92: BE A GREAT NEW DAD

By William Tiernan

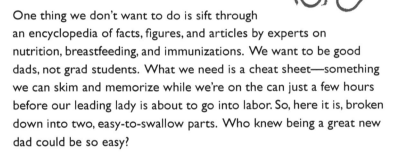

Browse the "Family" section of any commercial bookstore and you'll see dozens of books about parenting. But most new parent books are for women—*What to Expect When You're Expecting* and so on. What's a new dad to do?

One thing we don't want to do is sift through an encyclopedia of facts, figures, and articles by experts on nutrition, breastfeeding, and immunizations. We want to be good dads, not grad students. What we need is a cheat sheet—something we can skim and memorize while we're on the can just a few hours before our leading lady is about to go into labor. So, here it is, broken down into two, easy-to-swallow parts. Who knew being a great new dad could be so easy?

(Note: These tips are for the father of a brand-new infant; I don't know the first thing about parenting a teenager.)

Preparation

Get a job.

Get a second job, to pay for diapers.

Get in shape—babies move fast!

Get a decent car—one that won't spontaneously combust when rear-ended by a Chevy Tahoe.

Encourage mom to "express" milk and store it, so you'll be able feed the baby when she's exhausted.

Spring for a nice stroller—one that won't permanently weld your baby's shoulders to his or her ears.

Learn how to change a diaper; practice on your dog if you have one.

Locate the local zoo, library, and hospital.

Learn infant CPR.

Get life insurance.

Memorize some nursery rhymes.

Get a car seat—they won't let you leave the hospital without one.

Upon Arrival

Note: I use "her" because I have a little girl. In theory, these tactics work equally well for boys.

Deploy one of those baby stuffed animals that plays the guitar and sings Christmas carols.

When she's really screaming, hand her to mom.

Sing and dance with her.

Don't feed her hard candy the exact size of her throat.

Teach her how to clap.

Make her cool forts.

Teach her how to throw and catch.

When you put her down for a nap, let her cry; she'll fall asleep eventually.

Stop gambling, but play Powerball every once in awhile; if you win, you might be able to afford college in 20 years.

Change her poops immediately! Let's face it: You wouldn't want to scoot around in your own crap.

Take her to the circus, but don't sit in the first 20 rows; it will scare the shit out of her—literally.

Stop going to strip clubs—especially if you have a girl.

Take her to the park, and teach her how to go down the slide.

Take her to the local zoo and library.

Get out of your La-Z-Boy, and be a spotter for her as she crawls up the stairs!

Remember: Pens, knives, and forks are not toys.

Read to her—a lot. Get to know your board books.

Practice letters and numbers with her every day.

Get a digital camera; send pictures to her grandparents.

Cut your toenails and clean your feet; babies live close to the ground.

Plan a kick-ass mother's day!

Share your french fries with her.

Get her in the pool and on a bike.

Make sure her first word is "Daddy!"

Keep your job.

Keep your second job.

#93: Field Dress a Deer (or Other Large Animal)

By Jackson Landers

There you are, standing over the animal you managed to kill somehow or other. The sun is setting majestically behind you, and you are secure in the knowledge that you have obtained food from the wild through sheer pluck and skill.

Or have you? You can't just start nibbling at the hoof and keep going until you hit antlers. You'll find that the hunt was really the easy part. The real work begins after the shot.

To begin field dressing your kill, you'll first have to make an incision along the middle of the belly, starting at the sternum. The sternum is that bit of bone where the ribs come together at the bottom of the chest. You can find it by feeling the underside of the deer for where the soft stuff ends and the hard stuff begins. Be careful not to cut too deep. You want to cut through skin and muscle—at the most, you may pierce the thin membrane that holds the guts together. Under no circumstances should you cut into the actual intestines—that will make a dirty job even dirtier.

When your incision reaches the dangly parts, diverge into a "Y" shape around both sides of the genitals. Carve around the anus, and under the tail. Be careful not to go too deep in the backs of the legs—that's good meat, and you don't want to damage it.

Once you have the deer opened up, you need to get the guts out. Up until now, you've probably been careful not to get any blood on yourself, and you've been doing your best not to touch the actual cut-open parts at all. Well, that's too bad—you're going to be getting right in there now. First roll the deer over a bit to get the guts to spill out on their own as much as possible (downhill, please). Then, reach in there and get everything out of the chest cavity. Disconnect everything: esophagus, lungs, rumen, heart, etc. Again, be careful not to cut into any of the digestive organs, or you will regret it.

Try to pay attention while you're doing this; it's probably the best anatomy lesson you will ever get. See what your bullet or arrow did to the area it passed through. A good bullet will leave a path of destruction that turns the lungs into a pink, fluffy substance not unlike lumpy Jell-O. The wound channel should be several times the diameter of the bullet. If this is not the case, you need to go shopping for better ammo that transfers more energy into the target. Upgraded ammunition can be the difference between whether a slightly flubbed shot still manages to kill right away or results in eight hours of struggling to follow drops of blood through the woods in the freezing night. That's no picnic for the animal, either.

Also, note the preternatural hardness of the heart. Just brushing your fingers against it can give you the chills. That is one seriously strong muscle. This should inspire you to get off the couch more often and take better care of yours.

When it's time to disconnect the rear plumbing, be careful. You need to get everything out through the pelvis in one piece. You do not want poop on your meat. This is done by carefully cutting away all the tissue around the anus and the genitals. Then you need to carefully get it all out while it's still connected to the intestines, like some sort of grotesque reverse-birth out of a horror movie. It's a good idea to tie off the end of the intestines before pulling them through. A piece of string or some tough, fibrous dead grass will work in a pinch. Alternatively, you can crack the pelvis to remove all of this stuff. That can be easier if you have an appropriate tool, such as a hatchet.

Should you find that you have screwed up and opened up some part of the digestive tract, you will know it very quickly. In this event, you need to make sure to wash off the tenderloins and any exposed area of hindquarter before butchering later on. Otherwise, that meat will become contaminated with a foul taste and a mess of E. coli.

Once you've emptied the chest cavity, congratulations. You are officially a predator. You've field-dressed your kill and are well on your way to turning the deer into food. Proper butchering from this point on is a whole different process that I won't get into, save to tell you that it's not half as gross as the gutting process was, and you can probably muddle through it well enough by simply guessing what to do. You won't do an expert job without instruction, but you'll be able to put steaks on the grill.

If any part of these instructions disgusts you, you may want to reconsider your career as a hunter. Remember, every piece of meat on your plate goes through this process, whether you do it yourself or not—so if you really can't stomach it, it may be time to become a vegetarian.

#94: TELL IF SHE'S FAKING IT

By Alex Nowalk

Y ou really want to know whether your one-and-only is faking it? Here's the truth: You can't tell. Give up. If she's really good, sometimes *she* won't even be able to tell if she's faking it. How'd she get so good? By faking it with you—every time.

She compares you to one of those bendy straws. You're hung like an angry chipmunk. You'd make a good yardstick for a leprechaun. Sleeping with you is like having a sack of wet rice dropped on her, over and over. She's been humped more skillfully at the pound. At night, she takes candlelit baths just to be around something that doesn't go limp in five minutes. She likes it from behind; it's easier to fall asleep that way. When you talk her into doing it, she stares at the ceiling and pictures a Louisville slugger. You make toothpicks feel good about themselves.

Can't tell if you put the dew on her tulips? Don't whimper and cry like a girl. Just get in there, do your work, and punch out for the day. Time for a beer.

To Ask or Not To Ask:

If you've seen Meg Ryan's infamous fake-orgasm scene in *When Harry Met Sally* you may—like me—be haunted by an insatiable compulsion to find out the truth. The euphoric moments after sex are abruptly shattered by the inevitable question: "Did you...?" In my history as a man, I've sometimes asked, despite knowing I may seem needy or insecure. I've also refrained from asking, knowing I may seem cocky or callous. Here's what I've learned:

- If you want to know, but feel a bit foolish asking, there's an alternative. Pull her close and kiss the nape of her neck. If she's interested in making it a double-header, your first performance must not have been too shabby. Then again, maybe she's really unsatisfied, and she's hoping things will go better the second time around.

- If you've got the guts to ask, take her answer at face value. You don't want to throw a monkey wrench into the situation by coming across as mistrustful or accusing.

- Instead of asking whether she *did* or *didn't,* ask what she enjoyed the most. You're less likely to be unsure next time—and more likely to have a next time.

#95: CLOSE A DEAL

#96: INTERACT WITH CRACKHEADS

By Ryan Joe

The only people who don't love crack are the people who aren't on it. Unfortunately, that means we in polite society must learn to co-exist with our coarser brethren. Sometimes it seems that crackheads are just everywhere! What do you do?

Identifying a Crackhead

Crackheads have manic light dancing in their eyes. Often, they seem disassociated from their environments (usually a city street or alleyway, or a police cruiser). If you're waiting in line, they will cut it. Stay safe: assume that anyone who looks at you sideways is a crackhead.

What to Do

Avoid any confrontation with a crackhead. If a crackhead approaches you on an unlit city sidewalk, cross the street. If a crackhead cuts in front of you at the local deli, let him. If a crackhead is twittering around your apartment entrance, say, "Pardon me, good sir," and get indoors as quickly as possible.

Crackheads are not reasonable people. Do not make eye contact, as they might take offense. As a wise friend once said, "If you see someone coming toward you with 'crazy' in their eyes, walk the other way." Crackheads always have crazy in their eyes.

Unlike most people, crackheads don't think in terms of lawful consequences. They think in terms of crack.

What Not to Do

Don't invade the crackhead's physical space. There is a 99-cent pizza stand on the corner of 41st Street and Ninth Avenue in Manhattan. There is also a homeless shelter with lots of crack. Once, at the stand, I reached over a crackhead to grab the pepper flakes, and he popped me in the mouth. It was not a good experience, especially because I'd just finished grocery shopping and was carrying plastic bags full of eggs.

Don't insult the crackhead. A friend of mine was waiting for the train at 59th Street at four 'o' clock in the morning. A crackhead shuffled up to him and asked for change. My friend told the crackhead, "Get the heck away from me."

The crackhead bopped him on the head.

Fortunately, no one was hurt, but it was an unpleasant way for an evening to end.

What to Do if Avoiding Crackheads Is Impossible

Sometimes crackheads ask for money. Sometimes they demand money and pull out a knife. It's a good idea to keep a rolled-up wad of singles in your pocket. That way, you can throw it on the ground—as they stoop to pick it up, you have an opportunity to run away.

If you live in an urban area, you will often come home after a hard day's work to discover a crackhead sitting on your stoop. Generally, he'll let you pass without incident. But what if he grabs you?

The best thing to do is tell him, very loudly and authoritatively: "Get off." If that doesn't work, kick him in the nose. If you kick somebody in the nose, their eyes immediately tear, and they won't be able to see for a few minutes. You can then make your escape, and the crackhead won't be able to identify you later.

Perhaps you have a ball-peen hammer in your coat pocket. Don't use it. It's not worth the trouble. Even after you explain yourself to the police, you'll have wasted what should have been an educational afternoon at the Metropolitan Museum of Art.

Additionally, the crackhead might have friends who know where you live. This can pose numerous problems that you are not at all equipped to handle.

Crackheads Still Deserve Love

Following these simple strategies will protect you from unwanted interactions of all kinds. But while you're steering clear of crackheads, steer clear of hubris, too. You have your life, which doesn't involve crack, and they have theirs, which does. But no one's perfect, so give a crackhead a break now and then. You might even be surprised by how well these tactics work on non-crackheads in your life. Try them out on your mother-in-law at your next family function—you'll see what I mean.

#97: PLAY GOLF WITH TIGER WOODS

#98: ESCAPE AN ALIEN ABDUCTION

By Greg Kemp

Being abducted by aliens can be scary. Although it is believed that most alien abductions take place within six feet of your bed, it's impossible to predict the exact location or nature of the abduction. You must be prepared for anything. You might be confronted with one big alien with super-strength and horns, or 80 billion tiny one-celled aliens, operating together like a small twister. There might be bright lights, loud noises, and strong odors. Pain is possible, in the form of electric shock, temperature extremes, or headaches stemming from brain manipulations. Chances are the aliens have weapons like laser beams or poisonous fangs in their arsenal. They might have huge mouths, hell-bent on consuming you in a single bite to be excreted later, or they might blast you unconscious with an extraterrestrial goo-gun.

You want to avoid all of this mess. Your best bet is to try for an early escape. If they snatch you from your bed, grab a bedpost or other rigid structure. Kick, punch, and scream. Take note of their sensory organs. If they have a large eye or antennae, attack there. This will draw attention to yourself. If the aliens wanted abductions to be a public spectacle, they'd take people at supermarkets or at baseball games, and you don't see that very often. If you are unable to resist them, or if you find you've been teleported directly to the alien saucer, read on.

On the Saucer

One way or another, the aliens captured you. You're now on a saucer heading to their home planet at light speed. While traveling at light speed might feel cool, according to Einstein's theory of relativity, your loved ones back on earth are aging at a much faster rate and will soon be fossil fuels. You need to act quickly. Look for an escape pod, preferably one with an autopilot or a preprogrammed sequence for a quick Earth return. The location of the escape pod will probably be conspicuous to the aliens, but that doesn't mean it's obvious to you. Think. Do the aliens have eyes? They may see in much the way we do, so look for clear signage to the escape pod—something with contrasting colors and arrows. Perhaps there is a blinking sign.

Use common sense. If the aliens have big ears, don't look—listen. Don't be afraid to smell the walls searching for the escape pod, and you'd be foolish not to avail yourself of any brain wave signals you might be able to receive. During your search, you might find a teleportation device. It will probably be a clean room with a lot of lights and buttons, likely with an alien operator. Teleportation devices can be tricky to operate alone, so unless you can twist an alien's appendage while standing on a teleportation platform, you're better off using an escape pod.

If you can't find an escape pod, or you're locked in a cell, don't give up hope. There are still ways to get away. But you need to begin to collect information. Look for weaknesses you can exploit.

Alien Weaknesses

Remember, the laws of physics apply to aliens and earthlings alike. Machinery and electronics are vulnerable to tampering, and weapons can be taken. If an alien has a laser gun, take it and use it on him. If you see a self-destruct button on the ship, get to it. Threaten to blow up the ship if the aliens don't take you home.

Evaluate their physical prowess. Under the right circumstances, can you take them one on one? Can you take a hostage? If they are stringy and slippery like a wet noodle, don't wrestle, bite—but beware, they might be poisonous. Do they have hard shells or stingers? Humans are generally soft and don't fare well against creatures with exoskeletons or bodily weapons, so look for weak spots, like the sensory organs. Break off all antennae. Gouge soft-tissue receptors. Look for sexual organs and try to remove them. If your attacks fail, learn from your mistakes and keep trying. If you believe that you're doing everything right, yet you are unable to dominate an alien, consider the possibility that they might be reading your mind. Try not to think. Just act. You're a man. It's in your nature. But a word of caution: If the alien ship has robots or biomechanical creatures, stay away from them. They are dangerous to you and expendable to aliens. There is also the possibility the robots might be considered pets, and destroying an alien's pet will only get them mad.

The Long Journey to the Alien World

In the event that none of these tactics work, you need to reconsider strategies. You're trapped in a white cell unable to escape, and you're blasting through the solar system to some far away planet. Try communicating with your alien captors. Show them you are an intelligent life form. You might also try to seduce an alien. There are plenty of earthlings that would enjoy an alien sexual encounter. Perhaps you could use sex as springboard for an escape. If they appear offended, stop quickly. It might get you killed.

If you are able to communicate with the aliens, consider the possibility of negotiating. Perhaps they are only harvesting human limbs. It might be time to consider offering your arms and legs freely in exchange for a safe Earth return. If the time comes that you realize you're never going to get away, you've got to make a decision. Are you willing to accept life on an alien world? Will you be celebrated, or—more likely—studied and enslaved? Chances are you are not going to have a fulfilling life on an alien planet. You should probably take out as many aliens as you can, and sacrifice yourself in the name of humanity. Remember that tip earlier about looking for the sexual organs? Go after the soft stuff with a vengeance, singing the Star Spangled Banner the whole way.

#99: PARLAY

#100: ASK FOR DIRECTIONS

By Tom Treanor

on't.

#101: COUNT TO 101

101 THINGS SHOUT OUTS

No man is an island. That's why WEbook and the 28 authors of *101 Things Every Man Should Know how to Do* would like to thank the following people for their contributions to the ultimate manthology.

Thanks to Andrew Dixon Hutton, Jesse Lore, and Mark Kats, for wisecracks good enough to print. To all the WEbookers who threw in their two cents along the way—we couldn't have done it without you, and even if we could, we wouldn't want to.

Paul Peddrick and John Mitrione, our cover and layout designers—thank you both for converting our somewhat amorphous concept for the look and feel of *101 Things* into something seamless and logical—or at least something a few people we asked found amusing.

Thanks to Itai Kohavi for his vision of a place where writers could work together; to WEbook engineers Alon, Kimberly, and Tony, for making the vision real; and to Lark Dunham for keeping the whole engine running. For your support, ideas, and doodles, thanks to Amy Harrison, Danielle Farrah, John Meils, and Foundry Media's Yfat Reiss-Gendell. Thanks to Sue Heilbronner for having ideas, and for letting us tell her when they were stupid.

Thanks most especially to WEbook editor and perennial WEbook.com mascotrix Melissa Jones for spotting *101 Things* amidst the formative nubs of early WEbook.com, envisioning the power of the ultimate manthology, mediating between occasionally sparring boy- and girl-WEbookers during the writing, and lending the sheer force of her comically sardonic wit and charm to so many aspects of this little book.

WHAT IS WEBOOK ANYWAY?

WEbook.com is an online community where writers, readers, and "feedbackers" create great books and cast their votes to make their favorite undiscovered writers the next published authors.

WEbook is an innovative avenue for new writers to find an audience. WEbook.com satisfies the dreams of millions of aspiring authors and taps the wisdom of the crowd to create a unique new form of creative work: community-sourced books.

101 Things Every Man Should Know How to Do was written by 28 authors working on WEbook.com, with help from hundreds of other writers, readers, and feedbackers who shared their insights along the way. WEbook users gave the book the green light by voting for its publication in a site-wide competition. What's next? Thrillers, fantasy novels, mysteries, children's books, and more—all written, read, and selected by WEbook users.

WEbook.com is a whole new way of looking at how books are written and picked for publication. Learn more and see how you can be part of the revolution at www.WEbook.com.

ABOUT THE AUTHORS

ALEX NOWALK

Alex stands accused of sodomy, blasphemy, lechery, treachery, debauchery, arson, apathy, buggery, cannibalism, vanity, impersonation of a Dane, and being able to charm a woman to climax.

Alex invented cheese, sand, the rainforest, paper mills, the letter "C," soap-shaped famous historical figures, and David Hasselhoff.

Alex appreciates wine, whiskey, anyone who memorizes their favorite poem, women comfortable in old jeans and an oversized sweater, soccer, a fireplace, and people who own more books than movies.

ALYSSA J. WHITE

Alyssa has often been described as a nomad. She has had more zip codes and phone numbers than there are letters in her name. The hardest lesson she's learned is that she really cannot do everything on her own. The greatest triumph of her life is waking again every day, and realizing she has today and only today to live. This enables her to love every moment for what it is.

ANDREW GORI

Andrew Gori lives in San Francisco, CA.

BOBBY NELSON

Bobby is a high-school English teacher from Fairfax, Virginia, who has never lost a game of air hockey. He's made three people laugh so hard that they peed themselves. He also has an ongoing war with birds, and his favorite vacation spot is Detroit, Michigan. Yes, he's dead-serious.

BRIAN THOMPSON

Brian Thompson is the editor of the daily skeptical science humor blog The Amateur Scientist (www. amateurscientist.org). Among other places, his writing has appeared in "Yankee Pot Roast," "Turnrow," "Skeptical Inquirer," and various bathroom walls throughout the continental United States.

BRYAN BECHARD

Bryan is planning on becoming the 2010 World Series of Poker Champion by winning 11 bracelets in one year. He focuses his manly talents on destroying his opponents on the green felt, keeping a day job so he has a roof over his head, and helping to raise a four-month old (girl, but she already throws a mean right hook).

CURTIS MANCHESTER

Curtis Manchester studied philosophy and refrigerator repair at Southern Cross University. He currently works as a glass-bottom boat driver in Bermuda, where he lives with his wife Wesley and their two dobermans, Shepp and Moe.

Dorothy Carlow

Dorothy is waiting to be whisked away to Hawaii for a romantic vacation. Any takers?

Eden Anthony-Black

Eden Anthony-Black has often said that the story of her life would take up a whole week on one of those talk shows where people throw chairs at one another. She is addicted to caffeine, Chinese food, the Internet, Johnny Depp movies, and books. She collects frogs and merchandise from her favorite vacation spot.

Eden Anthony-Black lives in a small Oregon town with the love of her life and an alien who pretends to be a cat.

Eric Camarillo

Born and raised in Texas, Eric completely devours vampire novels; he has a hopeless addiction to teen fiction. He is currently attending the University of Texas at Austin, and hopes to be a world-famous writer.

Greg Kemp

Greg grew up in Melbourne, Florida. In the 1990s, he won an NCAA National Championship in soccer, became a licensed Professional Engineer, and graduated first at US Navy Deep Sea Dive School. Today he lives in Vienna, Austria—mopping floors, cleaning toilets, and cooking for two.

His latest creative project is a 2009 calendar of off-duty superheroes sporting Speedos. All proceeds will go to the Earthling Recovery Project, a non-profit organization that provides kick-ass parties for people who escaped an alien abduction.

JACKSON LANDERS

Jackson Landers hails from Charlottesville, Virginia—where he lives with his wife, Patricia, and their two children. A firm advocate of amateur everything, Landers blogs about ecology, politics, and firearms. As an Outward Bound alumnus, former Boy Scout, and ROTC cadet (medically disqualified before receiving a commission), he feels adequately qualified to instruct others in the manly arts.

JEFF BENDER

Jeff Bender's work has appeared in *Guernica* and *Captain Fiction*. He holds an MFA from Columbia University, where he received a Graham Fellowship and a Research Arts Fellowship. In 2008 he attended the Tin House Summer Writers Workshop in Portland, OR. He also won a fellowship to write at the Jentel residency in Banner, WY. Jeff is currently working on a novel called *The Weight*, about an ex-NCAA wrestler coming to terms with "life on the outside."

JOHN MEILS

John Meils is an editor at WEbook. Prior to joining the company, his shining moment in publishing was editing an autobiography by Marion Jones where she claimed, "I am against performance-enhancing drugs. I have never taken them, and I never will take them." John still believes Marion and is waiting for her comeback on the track.

KAREN GIBSON

Karen Gibson lives in the southeastern portion of the United States. She works as a nurse in the critical-care field and loves to write in her spare time. She is married and is the mother of two teenage boys: one destined to be the most sought-after professional gamer in the world, and the other slated to be the next "poster on the wall" rock star. She is very, very proud of both and hopes to be supported by one if not both of her sons in the beach house of her dreams in her later years. Fingers crossed!

NANCY R. HATCH

Nancy lives with her husband and cat, Tigger, on an island in the Chesapeake Bay. She has lived and worked up and down the Eastern Seaboard from New Jersey to South Carolina, as an attorney and in the non-profit world. She will be relocating to Florida shortly—as soon as the real estate market picks up—so that she can wear flip flops year-round, while sipping cold drinks on hot sand under swaying palms.

NANCY S. MURE

Nancy was born in Brooklyn, New York, the firstborn in a set of identical twins. She has authored eight children's stories and co-authored one. You may find out more about Nancy and her books at http://www.nancysmure.com or www.myspace.com/nancymure.

PADRAIG CARTY

Padraig is originally from Ireland, but he's been living in France since 1984, where he teaches English as a foreign language to poor unsuspecting students at a university in the Paris suburbs.

PATRICK VAN SLEE

Patrick was under the impression that the snacks were for everyone. He apologizes, he just saw that pile of bacon and figured he'd go ahead and grab a handful or two. He'd offer to give some of it back, but you don't even want to know what else has been in these pockets lately. Next time he will bring a ham platter or something.

R. ANDREW LAMONICA

R. Andrew Lamonica was born in the Midwest, where he also grew up and went to college. Then he visited Silicon Valley and decided to stay. Now, he lives in San Mateo and commutes on Highway 101 with all the other geeks. When he is not reading science fiction, playing games, taking things apart, watching a movie, or messing with his website, he writes code for Zazzle.com. The reason he writes more code than fiction is that programmers are not expected to be able to spell.

RYAN JOE

Ryan Joe is a policeman from the planet Thanagar. He lives in a satellite with other members of the Justice League community. His enemies include Lex Luthor, Black Manta, and the Joker.

RYAN PLACCHETTI

Ryan was born in a log cabin made of salvaged steel. The only utensil in his kitchen is a battle-axe, which he uses to spread butter over slabs of beef, because toast is for wusses. He only owns two pairs of shoes: boots and cowboy boots. He uses one pair for work, and both for kicking asses.

Ryan's role-models are Clint Eastwood, the Duke, and anybody who thinks that apostrophes were created by liberals to create a degree of separation between men and their possessions.

Ryan would like to dedicate his contributions to this book to his beloved gun.

STEVE CHANG

Steve, who now lives in Korea, is a busy and important person. Also, his opinion is more correct than yours.

TAHRA SEPLOWIN

Tahra lives in New York City.

TERESA SULTZBACH

Teresa Sultzbach grew up in Bedford, VA. She learned what every man should know how to do from her husband, a soldier in the United States army; her four sons; and her two great Danes. She currently lives in New Jersey and works in the least manly field there is—custom bra manufacturing.

Tom Treanor

Tom Treanor holds an MFA in creative writing from Columbia University. He lives in Brooklyn, NY, and he never, ever gets lost.

Vanessa Cobb

Born in Venezuela, Vanessa moved with her British family to England as a child. She now works as a presenter, business coach and writer, and lives with her teenage son in Devon. Her interest in car mechanics was sparked by one memorable journey from London to Glasgow in a 20-year-old VW Dormobile, during which the accelerator cable broke at full throttle and a wheel escaped from the rear axle. Since then, she has successfully bought and sold a fleet of road-worthy vehicles.

William Tiernan

William rarely leaves his basement apartment. He spends 18 hours a day trying to break the *Pitfall* world record on his Atari 2600. When he does come out, it's to go to the driving range, or to make a trip to the store to get another case of Mountain Dew.

READING GROUP QUESTIONS AND TOPICS FOR DISCUSSION

1. Throughout the book, many authors offer their advice under the banner of bolstering one's manliness. Do you think this is because masculinity is on the wane in general? And if so, where did it go? Was it stolen? By whom?

2. Reviewers have implied that Ryan Placchetti's essay, "How to Fight a Bear," is either a subversive critique of contemporary capitalism or a jab at professional wrestling. Which do you think it is? Could the author have made a stronger statement if he suggested fighting an endangered animal, like a manatee? A unicorn?

3. An obvious question you might have after reading 101 Things is: Where's the essay on the seasonal care of small trees and shrubs? Take a few minutes to discuss the risk/reward of pruning evergreen and deciduous branches in cold-weather climes. If this leads to a discussion of planting practices in frozen soil, run with it. If there is a ten-second silence after your reading group moderator reads this question, move on to the next one.

4. In Patrick Van Slee's "Choose Between the Woman You Love and Saving Thousands of Innocent Lives," the author recommends letting millions—even billions—of people die to save a single person. This scenario could result in significant intra-family coupling. Do you think this would be a good way to encourage evolution of the human species? How would you feel if your child was born with actual eyes in the back of its head?

5. Reviewers have likened the group dynamic described in "Host (and Win) an Atari Tournament" to the gladiator trials of ancient Rome. Do you agree that beating your friend at Dragster is the same as taking another man's life?

6. In his essay, "Rescue Chivalry." Alex Nowalk claims: "We can't all mount up and trot through downtown looking for someone to joust." But can't we? What if everyone mounted up and trotted downtown at the same time? There'd be plenty of people to joust each other then.

7. "Get Away with Almost Never Going to the Laudromat" offers some solid tips for getting the most out of your clothes. Do you think the author is also making a subtle case for water conservation? If so, do you feel it is okay for guys to get away with taking only a few showers per week?

8. In "Choose a New Career," by John Meils, he implies that men are happiest when they are drinking beer, having sex, or watching TV. Is Meils' assertion reductionist or an attempt at simplification on a meta level? Would you really prefer to spend your life drinking beer, having sex, or watching TV all the time? If you had to...oh forget it, just pass me a beer.

12134037R00140

Made in the USA
Lexington, KY
25 November 2011